Praise for *Democracy and the American Civil War*

"It is unfortunate that Alexis de Tocqueville died in 1859. His *Democracy in America* of 1835 was one of the most brilliant examinations of any society at any time in human history. What would he have thought about the American Civil War and the presidency of Abraham Lincoln? We will never know. Thankfully, this new volume, superbly edited by Kevin Adams and Leonne M. Hudson, draws us into the varied and vexed worlds of democracy during the nation's most grueling test with Tocquevillian talent. Any reader who wants to wrestle with democracy, race, and the Civil War will grab this volume."
—EDWARD J. BLUM, author of *Reforging the White Republic: Race, Religion, and American Nationalism, 1865–1898*

"At Gettysburg, Abraham Lincoln emphasized 'a new birth of freedom' for government of, by, and for the *people* (and that is the proposition he emphasized as he spoke, not the prepositions). The Civil War changed American democracy and American race relations in ways sweeping and subtle. From abolitionists and black troops to the Cherokee, from changing laws to growing lawlessness, this marvelous collection of essays examines ways in which Americans of the Civil War era tried—and sometimes failed—to live up to the ideals that Lincoln described, and gives us new ways to think about the times and the people at the heart of them."
—MICHAEL S. GREEN, author of *Lincoln and the Election of 1860*

"This slender volume illustrates that for all the recent work on emancipation during the Civil War era, imaginative scholars still draw fresh insights. Its coverage spans abolitionism, Abraham Lincoln, emancipation in the Cherokee Nation, the White Leagues in Reconstruction Louisiana, and the principle of *posse comitatus*. The relationship of race to democracy runs through all the essays. It is fitting that Kent State University's annual Symposium on Democracy, commemorating the events there in May 1970, sponsored these explorations. The contributors pay fitting tribute to the quest for a fuller and more inclusive democracy that each generation enriches with its blood."
—JOSEPH P. REIDY, Professor of History and Associate Provost, Howard University

"Reflections of the work and wisdom of five leading historians, the essays in this welcome volume probe and explain the most explosive racial controversies of the Civil War era: militant abolitionism, wartime emancipation, proud black soldiers, postwar Union military occupation, white resistance to Reconstruction, and the plague of ongoing racism. Together, they prove that American democracy's long quest for racial justice almost inevitably requires force and provokes violence."
—T. MICHAEL PARRISH, Baylor University

Democracy and the

American Civil War

Democracy and the American Civil War

✳ ✳ ✳

*Race and African Americans
in the Nineteenth Century*

✳ ✳ ✳

EDITED BY

KEVIN ADAMS

AND

LEONNE M. HUDSON

THE KENT STATE UNIVERSITY PRESS

KENT, OHIO

Portions of chapter 1 originally appeared in *A Companion to the U.S. Civil War*, edited by Aaron Sheehan-Dean, © 2014 John Wiley & Sons, Inc. Used by permission of John Wiley & Sons, Inc.

Portions of chapter 3 originally appeared on pages 74–92 of *Race and the Cherokee Nation: Sovereignty in the Nineteenth Century* by Fay A. Yarbrough, Copyright © 2008 University of Pennsylvania Press. Reprinted with permission of the University of Pennsylvania Press.

Cataloging information for this title is available at the Library of Congress.

20 19 18 17 16   5 4 3 2 1

Contents

Acknowledgments

It is only proper that we pause to recognize and acknowledge those persons who played a role in the success of the Symposium on Democracy and the publication of the book that followed. The planning for the symposium and the publication of the subsequent volume required the help and cooperation of several individuals. The members of the symposium planning committee would like to express their sincere gratitude to Lester A. Lefton, then president of Kent State University. His support for the symposium helped to guarantee its success. President Lefton fully understood that a university is a microcosm of society, in which democratic principles must be valued and protected. We also offer special thanks to Debra L. Berry of the president's office, who guided us around pitfalls and kept us on track without a word of complaint. When we found ourselves facing an uncertainty, Debra could always be counted on to provide calm and encouragement.

The work of the symposium planning committee was significantly eased by the outstanding support it received from Kent State University's Office of University Communications and Marketing, the Kent Student Center, the Department of History, the May 4 Visitors Center, and the Kent State University Bookstore. We would also like to thank the keynote speaker, panelists, and moderators of the sessions for their significant contributions to the program. The panel moderators, Lesley J. Gordon of the University of Akron and Kevin Adams and Leonne M. Hudson, both of Kent State University, added an important scholarly dimension to the symposium. We also extend a special note of appreciation to KSU's faculty, students, and staff, and to members of the community, for their support of and attendance at all or portions of the symposium.

The Kent State University Press supported the symposium project from the beginning and remained an invaluable resource throughout the planning process. The editors of this volume are especially indebted to Will Underwood, KSUP's director, and Joyce Harrison, its acquiring editor, for their commitment to the publication of these essays. We would like to thank the staff at the Press for making certain that this volume is a reflection of the high quality for which KSUP is known. We are grateful to the readers of this manuscript, Joseph P. Reidy and the other, anonymous, reader, for offering substantial suggestions for improving this work.

It is our hope that this volume will generate discourse on college and university campuses on the significance of tolerance, inclusion, and pluralism in a democratic nation.

Introduction

LEONNE M. HUDSON

The first May 4 Symposium on Democracy was held at Kent State University in April 2000. Carol A. Cartwright, then president of the university, established the symposium as a forum for scholarly discussion on the meaning of democracy in a pluralistic society. Through the symposium, the university emphasizes the promotion of civil discourse and the prevention of violent confrontations. Among the cornerstones of a democratic society are freedom of speech and freedom of assembly. If these are in any way circumscribed, America is diminished as a nation. By embracing the horrific events of May 4, 1970, Kent State University acknowledges in a very public way the unforgettable tragedy that occurred on its campus decades ago. The symposium also honors the memory of the four students who lost their lives on that day—Allison Krause, Jeffrey Miller, Sandra Scheuer, and William Schroeder—and of the nine others who were wounded when Ohio National Guardsmen opened fire on students protesting the war in Vietnam.

In 2011, against the backdrop of the nation's commemoration of the sesquicentennial of the Civil War, historians Leonne M. Hudson and Kevin Adams, along with Will Underwood, the director of the Kent State University Press, made a formal request to the university's administration to plan the Thirteenth Annual Symposium on Democracy. President Lester A. Lefton gave the green light to move forward, allowing the formation of the symposium planning committee of three. Its first order of business was to select a theme for the symposium. The committee decided on "Democracy and the American Civil War" in recognition of the 150th anniversary of the most devastating war in the history of the nation. We organized three panels and invited six leading scholars of the Civil War era to present their research. The distinguished historians who appeared on the symposium program were: Mitchell Snay of Denison University; John David Smith of the University of North Carolina at Charlotte; J. Matthew Gallman of the University of Florida; Mark Grimsley of Ohio State University; Stanley Harrold of South Carolina State University; and Fay A. Yarbrough of Oklahoma University (now at Rice University). Professors Adams and Hudson of Kent State University, along with Professor Lesley J. Gordon of the University of Akron, moderated the three sessions. The three-day symposium began on April 23, 2012, with a keynote address delivered by Pulitzer Prize–winning historical novelist Jeff Shaara. His address explored the reasons the Civil War continues to fascinate Americans and what is it about the war that makes it such an enduring phenomenon. Shaara's oration received an enthusiastic reception from the audience.

Although the Frenchman Alexis de Tocqueville declared, after touring the United States in the 1830s, that "America is the most democratic country in the world," groups then living on the margins of U.S. society, such as Native Americans, women, and blacks, would not have agreed with his assessment. Racial slavery, the defining characteristic of the American South, remained firmly entrenched as the nation moved into the latter years of the antebellum period. In 1837, Senator John C. Calhoun of South Carolina proudly announced that slavery was "a positive good." Another famous American had a completely different view of the peculiar institution, however: Frederick Douglass no doubt understood the contradiction between democracy and slavery as well as any of his contemporaries. Douglass, the preeminent leader of his race, reminded the nation in 1852 that the slave was "the constant victim" of American injustice. Bedeviled by political and insurrectionist attacks against their unique way of life, Southerners redoubled their efforts to preserve their labor system at all costs.

With the benefit of hindsight, it would not be an exaggeration to conclude that Abraham Lincoln's election to the presidency in 1860 marked the beginning of the end for slavery. His victory triggered the disintegration of the nation, as Southern states responded to it by drafting ordinances of secession. Before the parade of secession ended, eleven states had join forces to create a new Confederate republic. Secession forced the federal government to grapple with the greatest threat to American democracy in the nation's history; Lincoln's administration responded by refusing to accept the disintegration of the republic. During the Civil War that resulted, courageous people on both sides waged a colossal struggle, desperately attempting to stamp the pages of history with the seal of victory. For four tumultuous years, the fate of the nation rested on the shoulders of hundreds of thousands of Union and Confederate soldiers. President Lincoln stood at the center of the conflict, and his idealism regarding democracy, combined with his brilliant leadership, helped save the Union for future generations. The essays in this volume focus on the unifying themes of democracy and race during and after the Civil War. The scholars of this collection remind us of the historical importance of democracy and the complexity of issues of race during the nineteenth century and beyond.

The first essay in this book, contributed by Stanley Harrold, places abolitionism at the forefront of the reform crusade during the antebellum years. Social history as a field of study is important for our understanding of both the antislavery impulse and the civil rights movement of the 1960s. Asserting that one of the objectives of humanitarian crusades is to "expand democracy," especially for the less fortunate and the downtrodden, Harrold points out that the reformism of the nineteenth century continued into the twentieth. Of all the social movements to arise in the United States, the drive to end slavery, which one historian called the "ultimate reform," was the most violent and dangerous. Abolitionists, who were a diverse group, welcomed the Civil War as a necessary conflict to end slavery. Harrold maintains that "it is not difficult to establish that abolitionists (fanatics or not) had an important role in bringing on the Civil War and helped shape Union emancipatory policies during the war." The anti-slavery crusaders enthusiastically greeted the president's Emancipation Proclamation and the enlistment of black men into the Union army. With increasing frequency, the abolitionists called on Lincoln to place the government "on the side of freedom." A glaring failure of the abolitionists was their inability to secure equal rights for African Americans after the war. Harrold concludes that it took a hundred years and another revolution before blacks could enjoy the full benefits of citizenship, although he notes that incidents such as the shooting of an unarmed black teenager in Ferguson, Missouri, in 2014 raise doubts about the extent of racial progress in American society.

The essay by John David Smith follows Abraham Lincoln on his path of "emancipation and black recruitment" during the Civil War. Like many of his contemporaries, Lincoln harbored racist views, and did not favor the immediate abolition of slavery. However, he did believe slavery to be a morally offensive institution that robbed African Americans of their humanity, and had long advocated a gradual program of emancipation of slaves, with compensation for their owners. Once inaugurated as president, Lincoln's first priority was the preservation of the Union. Although he knew that he could use the power of that office to destroy the pernicious system of slave labor, he feared that immediate and universal abolition would alienate slave owners in the border states of Delaware, Kentucky, Maryland, and Missouri, which were still loyal to the Union, and continued to look into a process of gradual emancipation. By the summer of 1862, however, he had shifted his approach toward more immediate emancipation, believing that such a step would sow discord within the Confederate states and allow former slaves to fight for the North.

Smith claims that Lincoln, the consummate politician, approached military emancipation in a calculating and methodical manner. The liberation of the bondsmen culminated in the Emancipation Proclamation, which, among other things, provided for the enlistment of black men into the United States Army. Not surprising, Lincoln's decision to allow black enlistment produced consternation and controversy in several quarters. Many Northerners responded to the mustering of blacks into the Union army with a disapproval tinged with racism. Smith reminds us that Lincoln's decision to free and arm the slaves represented a new political reality: that "the door for future racial equality and citizenship" for African Americans had been opened. The colored troops endured discrimination and poor treatment, which "largely mirrored their status in American society at large." Once in the war, they "served well—in combat," confirming that they were worthy of Lincoln's investment in them as soldiers. Smith concludes that Abraham Lincoln and the United States Colored Troops were inextricably bound together and that both have earned their place in the history of the Civil War and the history of America.

Race, identity, and power all converge in the essay by Fay A. Yarbrough. She discusses the place of men and women of African descent in the Cherokee Nation of Oklahoma after the Civil War. The Cherokees had a history of slave ownership dating back to the early years of the nineteenth century; by the eve of the Civil War, as Yarbrough notes, black slaves constituted nearly twenty percent of the population of the Cherokee Nation. After the war, these freed people faced a daunting challenge to affirm their rights as full citizens in the Cherokee Nation. The Cherokees believed that there was a connection between their own survival and the adoption of white culture. In the duplication of Southern white culture, therefore, they codified the social and political inferiority of blacks into Cherokee law, relegating them to second-class status. Yarbrough states that the Cherokees "identified more closely with whites, not just because of physical appearance but also in their perception of the linkage between race and power and success." While intermarriage between whites and Cherokees was an accepted practice in the Cherokee Nation, intermarriage between blacks and Cherokees was prohibited, and the enforcement of this prohibition in the Cherokee Nation underscores Cherokee attitudes about race. "By freeing their slaves and including them in the nation's citizenry," Yarbrough contends, "Cherokees had to rethink definitions of citizenship and Cherokee identity." She concludes that the relationship between African Americans and Cherokees remains tenuous to this day.

Kevin Adams begins his essay with an explanation of the historical origin of *posse comitatus* and goes on to explore its use during Reconstruction and after. One of the historic roles of the United States Army has been that of protecting the democratic values of Americans. Most Americans of the nineteenth century were unaware of the army's service as a *posse comitatus*, or institution of domestic law enforcement. After the Civil War, the U.S. Army went south as an "army of democracy." Dormant for many years, *posse comitatus* became a topic of conversation in 1867, when Congress took control of reconstructing the nation. Adams notes that *posse comitatus* was much more than an esoteric term during the postwar years, instead becoming a concept "absolutely central to the success of Reconstruction on the ground" in the South. Noting that many scholars, including military historians, have neglected to fully explore the connection between *posse comitatus* and Reconstruction, he asserts that by placing *posse comitatus* in its proper "legal and constitutional context," a better understanding of the intervention of the United States Army in the South during the Reconstruction era will emerge.

The first use of *posse comitatus* after the Compromise of 1877 was the deployment of troops on behalf of black students in Little Rock, Arkansas, in 1957. Adams maintains that a close examination of Section 15 of the Army Appropriations Act reveals that it allowed for the "use of the army as domestic law enforcement," most notably in the field of civil rights. He contends that despite congressional limitations on *posse comitatus,* the president had and has the authority to protect the civil rights of the nation's citizens through military intervention. By using *posse comitatus* during the civil rights movement, the federal government sought to fulfill the promise of democracy in places that had a long history of circumventing equality and justice for African Americans.

Mitchell Snay examines race and class in his piece on the White Leagues of Louisiana during the postwar years. The Leagues, which started in 1874, aimed their venom at Republicans and African Americans of the Bayou state. The Civil War and Reconstruction were the catalysts for the expansion of democratic rights for African Americans in Louisiana. In an effort to halt this change and deprive African Americans of their citizenship rights, the White Leaguers carried out a campaign of violence and intimidation against them. This repression of black Louisianans did not subside with the collapse of Reconstruction in 1877. Snay sees the wave of violence perpetrated against African Americans partially as a continuation of the activities of the Ku Klux Klan, but he also points out the tension between rural Leaguers and their brethren in the city of New Orleans. Class differences among white Louisianans manifested themselves in the formation of political and agrarian organizations before the turn of the century. The entrenchment of racism in Louisiana signaled difficult days ahead for African Americans of that state as they continued their push for equal civil and political rights. According to Snay, "the racism so deeply embodied in the White Leagues survived into the agrarian crusades of the late nineteenth century."

The origin of democracy in the United States can be traced to the revolutionary era of the 1770s. Under the banner of "life, liberty, and the pursuit of happiness," the young nation struggled to affirm the freedom of its citizens. More than eighty years later, the Civil War severely tested America's democratic institutions and its constitutional system of government. The triumph of the Union confirmed that the nation was indivisible and that it would remain an organic whole. According to the historian Benjamin Quarles, the Civil War successfully enlarged "the compass of American democracy." Therefore, our democracy must be defended and protected for the benefit of all Americans and for future generations.

Morality, Violence, and Perceptions of Abolitionist Success and Failure from Before the Civil War to the Present

STANLEY HARROLD

Reform movements are interwoven into American culture. Such lasting American characteristics as distrust of government, regional differences, millennialist religion, natural rights theory, individualism (and fears of it), class divisions, and republicanism are tied to the nation's reform impulse. Reform springs from a variety of motives and social classes. It aims to increase morality, help the downtrodden, and expand democracy. It also has ups and downs, which can lead reformers *and* historians to varying and contradictory conclusions regarding a particular movement's success or failure. Especially in regard to the pre–Civil War movement to abolish slavery, the issue of violent means has had a central role in determining such conclusions. Certain other American reform movements, such as prohibition, labor organization, and civil rights, are likewise, to varying degrees, associated with violence. But because of abolitionism's relationship to the antebellum sectional struggle, the Civil War, and Reconstruction, issues of violence have most affected perceptions of it.

A major American reform era began during the 1810s and continued into the Civil War years. Antebellum reformers hoped to transform the country. A wide range of campaigns flourished: to distribute Bibles, save souls, end mail delivery on Sundays, improve eating habits, discourage alcohol consumption, promote public education, make the penal system more humane, end the flogging of sailors, and raise the status of women. Of them all, the movement to abolish slavery was by far the oldest, largest, most vociferous, and most threatening to the status quo. As historian Ronald G. Walters put it more than thirty years ago, abolitionists "envisioned themselves as part of some great procession stretching across the centuries—soldiers in the long march of Protestantism, Reason, Progress, [and] Democracy."[1] Self-righteous, deadly serious, self-critical, and not easily disillusioned, abolitionists embraced reform as the hard work of a lifetime. They equated failure with damnation.

6

In 1775, Philadelphia Quakers organized the first abolition society in the world. Although this society failed to persist in its original form, the early abolitionists succeeded in fewer than thirty years. Through peaceful means, they helped end slavery in the northeast—immediately in a few states and gradually in the rest. This success, together with the ban on slavery in the Northwest Territory encoded in the Northwest Ordinance of 1787, helped make slavery a North-South sectional issue. So did Eli Whitney's 1793 invention of the cotton gin. Before this invention, most Americans outside South Carolina and Georgia assumed slavery would fade away. But as the cotton gin sped processing of short-staple cotton, cultivation of the crop expanded in Virginia, North Carolina, Georgia, and South Carolina, and spread westward into Alabama, Mississippi, Louisiana, Tennessee, Arkansas, and (eventually) Texas. As a result, black slavery became the direct basis of the South's economy and indirectly essential to the economy of much of the Northeast.

Meanwhile, religious revivalism, northern self-interest, and black demands for racial justice expanded abolitionism. By 1830, a more radical movement had emerged. Led by William Lloyd Garrison and his weekly newspaper, *The Liberator,* "modern abolitionists" called for the immediate, *peaceful,* abolition of slavery in the South and equal rights for African Americans. In 1833, Garrison organized these proponents of immediate abolition as the American Anti-Slavery Society (AASS), which sought to convince Northerners and Southerners that, for the sake of their souls and to avoid massive slave revolt, human bondage had to end quickly. In the AASS's 1833 Declaration of Sentiments, immediatists not only limited themselves to nonviolent means of reform, they pledged to discourage slaves from rising against their masters. By the late 1830s, as abolitionists divided over tactics, the Garrisonian faction embraced a more extreme form of pacifism known as nonresistance.[2]

Yet from the late 1820s onward, some abolitionists justified violence against slavery. Black abolitionist David Walker, in his *Appeal to the Colored Citizens of the World,* published in Boston in 1829, called on enslaved black men to rise up against masters who assaulted their wives and daughters. By the early 1840s, abolitionists were going beyond rhetoric, arming themselves as they helped slaves escape their masters. Prominent among this group were Charles T. Torrey, a white abolitionist from Massachusetts who lived in Washington, D.C., during the early 1840s, and his associate Thomas Smallwood, a free black Washington native. The two men organized an escape network that stretched from northern Virginia to Canada, and Torrey (at least) carried pistols.[3]

By 1849, the prominent black abolitionist Frederick Douglass had shed his former pacifism, declaring: "I should welcome the intelligence tomorrow . . . that the slaves had risen in the South, and that . . . sable arms . . . were engaged in spreading death and destruction there." By the early 1850s, radical political abolitionists, centered in western New York and led by Gerrit Smith, asserted that violence had to play a role in ending slavery. "If the American revolutionists had excuse for shedding but one drop of blood," Smith exclaimed in 1850, "then have the American slaves excuse for making blood flow 'even to the horse-bridles.'" Beginning in 1855, fighting between antislavery and proslavery forces in Kansas Territory played a role. Long-time pacifist Angelina Grimké Weld embraced "baptiz[ing] liberty in blood [in Kansas] if it must be so." In 1856, Smith observed, "There is not virtue enough in the American people to bring slavery to a bloodless termination; and all that remains for them is to bring it to a bloody one."[4]

During the late 1850s, some nonresistants changed their minds about violent means. In 1857, Henry C. Wright, a Garrisonian pacifist, told the Massachusetts Anti-Slavery Society that "We owe it as our duty to ourselves and to humanity to excite every slave to *rebellion* against his master." Such rhetoric was not good enough for John Brown. Emerging from a Boston Garrisonian meeting in early 1859, Brown scoffed: "Talk! talk! talk!—that will never set the slave free."[5] These violent abolitionist tendencies culminated, later that year, in Brown's raid on Harpers Ferry, Virginia. The raid, along with the election to the presidency of Abraham Lincoln—an antislavery (but not abolitionist) Republican—in November 1860, helped push the Lower South into secession between December 1860 and February 1861.[6]

By the time of his execution in December 1959, if not earlier, John Brown had come to believe that *only* bloodshed could reform America. A decade earlier, Karl Marx had reached a similar conclusion regarding all capitalistic societies. By the late 1850s, Garrison and highly influential evangelical Lewis Tappan were in a minority of abolitionists who clung to nonviolence.

As the seven Lower South states seceded from the Union during the winter of 1860–61, following Lincoln's election in November 1860, most abolitionists preferred to let them go. But peace principles did not shape their outlook. Instead abolitionists believed it was preferable to let the Lower South states leave the Union than for Congress to enact a proslavery compromise to entice them back in. Abolitionists also hoped that the secession of the Lower South would provoke a successful slave rebellion, accomplishing the destruction of slavery. Douglass voiced these views when he declared in January 1861 that "if the Union can only be maintained by new concessions to the slaveholders; if it can only be stuck together and held together by a new drain on the negro's blood; if the North is to forswear the exercise of all rights incompatible with the safety and perpetuity of slavery . . . then will every right-minded man and women in the land say, let the Union perish, and perish forever."[7]

This abolitionist point of view evaporated in April 1861 with the Confederate attack on Fort Sumter and Lincoln's call for Union troops. In response to these events, many abolitionists endorsed a war they believed would end slavery. Henry B. Stanton, an AASS stalwart during the 1830s and a political abolitionist during the 1840s, told his wife, Elizabeth Cady Stanton, "I hear Old John Brown knocking on the lid of his coffin & shouting 'Let me out,' 'let me out!!' The doom of slavery is at hand. It is to be wiped out in blood. Amen!" Oliver Johnson, a Garrisonian journalist, remarked more directly: "In spite of every effort to control or qualify it, it must be, essentially, a war of freedom against slavery." The next day Garrison advised Johnson, "It is no time for minute criticism of Lincoln, Republicanism, or even the other Parties, now that they are fusing for a death grapple with the Southern slave oligarchy; for they are instruments in the hands of God to carry forward and help achieve the great objectives of emancipation.... the war is fearfully to scourge the nation, but mercy will be mingled with judgment, and grand results are to follow."[8]

After the Union defeat at Bull Run, Douglass hoped northerners would "now call not only for vengeance and righteous retribution [against the Confederacy], but for ... the abolition of slavery. ... by the simple process of calling upon the blacks of the South to rally under the Star-Spangled Banner, and work and fight for freedom." At about the same time, Tappan told the American Peace Society that, while "all war was contrary to the Gospel, unnecessary, and wicked," the continued existence of slavery would be worse. For the Union government to give up fighting, Tappan noted, would "perpetuate human bondage, the chief cause of the war."[9]

As time passed, even abolitionists more committed to pacifism than Garrison and Tappan began to lean toward such sentiments. Sarah Grimké, a Quaker, had for decades opposed all violence, yet in November 1863, she told Garrison, "This war, the holiest ever waged, is emphatically God's war; and whether the nation will or not, He will carry it on ... until every American enjoys the rights claimed for him in our Declaration of Independence." Grimké's brother-in-law Theodore Weld, another long-term pacifist, likewise declared, "I profoundly believe in the righteousness of such a war as this, on its anti-slavery side." To a friend, he added that "[we] exault ... in this mighty Northern uprising, not withstanding its mixtures of motives and base alloys and half truths and whole lies. ... The elements of a vast moral revolution are all aglow in the surging mass. A national religious revival better deserving the name, than anything that has preceded it. Simple right is getting such a hearing as never before on this continent."[10]

Abolitionists increasingly pressed a reluctant Lincoln to announce that Union armies fought for black emancipation as well as to preserve the Union; they also argued that the Northern armies must enlist black men. "The war at its foundation is all about the black man," stated Elizure Wright, an independent political abolitionist, in May 1861, " ... and before the war is through the black man is almost certain to be fighting for himself." That June, Douglass urged abolitionists to "give ... no support or continence" to the Union war effort "until the government shall ... place itself openly and unequivocally on the side of freedom." At an abolitionist meeting on July 4th at Framingham, Massachusetts, Stephen S. Foster, a Garrisonian, urged abolitionists to convince Northerners that the Union had to make emancipation a war aim as a means of defeating the Confederacy. The North, he maintained, could not "crush out treason without hurting the traitors," and the way to hurt slaveholders was "to . . . dash against [slavery] with all the force of its own violence."[11]

Through such words, and through lobbying the president and Congress, abolitionists helped shape Lincoln's Emancipation Proclamation and the Union decision to enlist black troops. They also led Northern public opinion toward accepting these measures. Abolitionist men and women also led by example, going to the South to serve among former slaves on plantations and in refugee camps and working as nurses, administrators, and teachers. Black and white abolitionists raised black Union troops, and younger white abolitionist men led them in battle. Abolitionists also urged the formation of what in 1865 became the Freedmen's Bureau. They inspired the Thirteenth Amendment, shaped the Fourteenth, and advocated the Fifteenth, amendments that, among other provisions, ended slavery, recognized black civil rights, and gave black men the right to vote.[12]

By January 1862, some abolitionists believed the Civil War would end their struggle by ending slavery. They prepared to stop agitating in the North and lobbying in Washington. J. Miller McKim, a Garrisonian from Philadelphia, assumed slavery would disintegrate as a byproduct of war, making further abolitionist effort superfluous. A month later, Maria Weston Chapman, a close associate of Garrison, agreed. She believed younger generations would overpower slavery's legacies.[13]

By the end of 1863 (nearly a year after the issuance of the Emancipation Proclamation), abolitionists had begun to congratulate themselves on their success. In November, Garrison, anticipating the AASS's thirtieth anniversary meeting, credited the organization with inducing Lincoln's Emancipation Proclamation. "The Society will have the sublime privilege to announce, as the result, primarily of its disinterested, patriotic, and Christian labors," Garrison concluded, "the emancipation of THREE MILLION THREE HUNDRED THOUSANDS SLAVES, by the fiat of the American Government on the 1st of January last." At the anniversary meeting, Mary Grew, of the Philadelphia Female Anti-Slavery Society, proclaimed: "The work of the American abolitionists is accomplished." She then added, "Verily, it is fitting that we . . . grasp one another's hands in fraternal congratulation." Abolitionist self-congratulation continued into the postwar period. When he ceased publishing *The Liberator* in December 1865, Garrison acknowledged that "a mighty work of enlightenment and regeneration" remained to be accomplished in the South. He nevertheless declared the abolitionist objective, "the extermination of chattel slavery, . . . gloriously consummated."[14]

Nearly a decade later, Douglass sent a letter to the aging abolitionists attending an 1874 reunion in Chicago. "No class of the American people," he wrote, "can look toward the sunset of life with a larger measure of satisfaction than the Abolitionists." According to Douglass, "they ha[d] done a great work—*the* great work of the century. They ha[d] given the American slaves their freedom and the American people the possibility of a country." The abolitionists had, in Douglass's estimation, "delivered." They had imperiled "everything but honor for the freedom of others." Douglass's audience did not need this encouragement. In reminiscences published between the late 1860s and the 1880s, abolitionists took pride in having brought on a war that led to emancipation. They portrayed themselves as heroes in a successful struggle against slavery. "When all the animosities excited by the great conflict have passed away, and the historian comes to tell the story with perfect impartiality," declared the abolitionist journalist Oliver Johnson in 1879, "the character and fame of Garrison will shine forth with new lustre. . . . as the founder and the leader of the movement by which American slavery was exterminated, and the fetters of four million of American slaves were forever broken." Another abolitionist journalist, James Freeman Clarke, proudly asserted in 1883, "In every way we have reason to be thankful for the great progress throughout the whole Southern country by the white and the colored people."[15]

Despite such self-congratulation, however, many abolitionists, black and white, came to believe they had failed to accomplish one, or perhaps both, of their major goals. They lamented that the termination of legal slavery had not led white Americans to accept equal rights for African Americans.[16] Most surviving abolitionists concluded that, while they had secured emancipation, they had failed to bring about moral reformation in white opinion. Returning to pacifism, abolitionists (in contrast to John Brown and Karl Marx) asserted that only peaceful means could produce such a reformation.

A few abolitionists had never deserted pacifism. As early as November 1861, Parker Pillsbury, a Garrisonian loyalist turned critic, denounced the Lincoln administration for coming to "this doctrine of the abolition of slavery at last as 'a *military necessity.*'" Pillsbury claimed (incorrectly) that military emancipation "never was successfully done, and while God lives and reigns, it never can be done," and contended that violent abolition was "the most God-insulting doctrine ever proclaimed." In January 1862, abolitionist journalist Lydia Maria Child worried that if emancipation resulted from "a 'war necessity,' everything *must* go wrong [because] there is no heart or conscience on the subject."[17]

In December 1863, two colleagues of Pillsbury and Child, Stephen Foster and Abigail Kelley Foster, warned that a successful Union war for emancipation would not guarantee equal rights for African Americans. Stephen claimed that Lincoln cared only "for the white man and the perpetuity of the Federal Government," while Abigail added that Northern opinion on black emancipation had changed "not from the highest motives" but from "military necessity." Douglass, despite his support for the war, shared some of Foster's concerns. While admitting that "I am one of those who believed that it is the mission of this war to free every slave in the

United States," he predicted that ending "prejudice against color" and gaining full political rights for black men would be more difficult.[18]

In June 1865 (shortly after the formal end of the war), Stephen Foster pointed to the gap between legal emancipation for slaves and their full assimilation into American society at the thirty-second anniversary meeting of the AASS. Reminding his associates that they had once "discarded the idea of forcible emancipation," he noted that the U.S. victory in the war had produced "none other than emancipation effected by physical violence." In "a forced emancipation, the moment the force is withdrawn, the crime will be repeated," he warned. "The only hope for the negro is in imprinting the law of justice upon the American heart." Five months later, Henry C. Wright echoed this sentiment, declaring that "military power" could never protect "human rights." Slavery had died, but "its *spirit* and its *results* live[d]." The abolitionist orator Wendell Phillips added a further warning in 1869: "Once let public thought float off from the great issue of the war," he asserted, "and it will take perhaps more than a generation to bring it back again. . . . Unless some remedy is devised, the negro will stand in peril and use his rights only at great personal hazard for many years to come." Many abolitionists argued that no true reformation of sentiment could occur when military strategy alone had led a Northern majority to support emancipation. Black rights, they predicted, would exist in the South only so long as military force protected them.[19]

As white Southern resistance to Reconstruction and black rights intensified, abolitionists' doubts about the success of their cause proliferated. Samuel Joseph May, who before the war had worked with Garrison and Gerrit Smith, charged that "our Government has been guilty of great injustice to the colored population of the South, who were all loyal [to the Union] throughout the war." African Americans, according to May, "should not have been left as they have been, in a great measure, at the mercy of their former masters." In 1874, Garrison asserted that efforts at reconciliation between the North and South promoted "the old dragon spirit of slavery, and perpetuat[ed] caste distinctions by laws." In 1876, Amos Dresser, who had been an early associate of Theodore Weld and had suffered a beating by a proslavery mob in Tennessee, added: "There yet remains a great work to be done to eradicate the spirit of slavery and the spirit of caste so deeply rooted in the heart, a work that can be fully accomplished only by the Gospel of our Lord Jesus Christ." That same year, while acknowledging that the Civil War had produced emancipation, Garrison asked, "What special credit may we [abolitionists] claim for this, seeing it was done expressly as a 'military necessity, in order to preserve the Union, and not because of the wrongfulness of oppression?" He advised abolitionists, "If we rejoice at all, let it be with contrite hearts that we have not been utterly consumed."[20]

Abolitionists either forgot or repudiated their support of military emancipation. In 1884, Douglass summed up their retrospective lament: "Liberty came to the freedmen of the United States not in mercy, but in wrath, not by moral choice but by military necessity, not by the generous action of the people among whom they were to live, and whose good-will was essential to the success of the measure, but by strangers, foreigners, invaders, trespassers, aliens, and enemies. . . . Nothing was to have been expected other than what has happened." Unlike Douglass, Kentucky abolitionist Cassius M. Clay had never been a pacifist. He briefly served as a Union general. But in 1886, he agreed with Douglass concerning the ineffectiveness of force. Clay observed that "force has been tried" and only enhanced white Southern resistance to black rights. According to Clay, abolition by war "was the chief cause of [white] southern solidity [*sic*]" during Reconstruction. He believed that "the disease [of racism was] too great and widespread for such remedy."[21]

From the late nineteenth century to the mid–twentieth century, historians overlooked both the abolitionists' impact during the Civil War and their second thoughts about the war. Largely because of the North-South reconciliation effort that began after the war, even late-nineteenth-century historians who recognized the role of abolitionists in causing the Civil War ignored their role during the war. Because of their racial bias and support for sectional reconciliation, even historians who favored the Union cause ignored the war's failure to secure lasting rights for African Americans.[22]

Since then, most writing on abolitionists has centered on the antebellum years. Those were the years during which the North and South moved toward war. And into the 1960s, despite their lack of attention to the abolitionist role during the Civil War, historians asserted a major abolitionist role in causing the war and thereby achieving emancipation. In 1892, James Ford Rhodes wrote about abolitionists in the first volume of his seven-volume *History of the United States from the Compromise of 1850*. Asking readers to "picture . . . [a] process of [abolitionist] engagement, of discussion, of persuasion, going on for twenty-five years, with an ever-increasing momentum," Rhodes concluded that " . . . we cannot resist the conviction that this agitation had its part, and a great part, in the first election of Lincoln." During the 1930s, historians Gilbert H. Barnes and Dwight L. Dumond asserted that the morally oriented abolitionism of the 1830s underlay and lived on in the antislavery politics of the Republican Party.[23]

As Barnes conceived it, "Throughout the later agitation from the [eighteen] forties to the 'sixties the doctrine of the antislavery host . . . continued in the moral tenets of the original antislavery [abolitionist] creed. In this crusading spirit their support of men and measures was constantly maintained until 1860, when, county by county, the antislavery [abolitionist] areas gave Abraham Lincoln the votes which made him President." Dumond went further, portraying Lincoln *as* an abolitionist, "thoroughly sound on the fundamental principles of abolitionist doctrine." According to Dumond, those principles were "that the subject of slavery was not a domestic concern of the Southern States, that it was a moral and political evil which menaced the rights of free men, was contrary to the principles of the Declaration of Independence and a violation of eternal principles of right."[24]

The *revisionist* and *consensus* schools of historians, which dominated studies of the Civil War era during the long period from the 1920s through the 1950s, did not share the positive view of the impact of abolitionists before the Civil War asserted by Rhodes, Barnes, and Dumond. Instead, the reactionary revisionist and conservative consensus historians held abolitionists to have been "irresponsible fanatics," who irrationally held slaveholders responsible for *Northern* social evils. In 1942, revisionist Avery O. Craven stated that the movement "arose out of apprehension engendered by changes" caused by industrialization in New England and New York. Slaveholders, in Craven's view, did "scapegoat service" for class antagonism against a new Northern business "aristocracy."[25]

Still, these anti-abolitionist historians agreed that abolitionists had played a major role in pushing the country toward sectional war. According to Craven, "Abolition[ists] threatened to produce a race problem which had in large part been solved by the institution of slavery, and caused a move for [Southern] independence." In *The Civil War and Reconstruction* (published in 1937 and the best-selling Civil War history textbook of its time), James G. Randall wrote that abolitionists introduced "the avenging force of Puritanism in politics" and argued that it was "a major cause of the conflict."[26] The difference between the revisionist and consensus historians on the one side and Rhodes, Barnes, and Dumond on the other was that the former groups believed the war to have been a mistake. They regarded slavery as a "benign" institution that would have ended peacefully if not for abolitionist agitation.

It took the civil rights movement and Kenneth M. Stampp's *The Peculiar Institution,* published in 1956, to encourage historians to reject this particularly negative view of abolitionists. Stampp portrayed slavery as a brutal system of forced labor. He quoted a North Carolina master, who asserted that "slavery and Tyranny must go together and . . . there is no such thing as having an obedient and useful slave, without the painful exercise of undue and tyrannical authority. . . . The power of the Master must be absolute, to render the submission of the slave perfect." In this context, abolitionist demands for an end to slavery seemed rational rather than irrational. Not long after the publication of Stampp's book, boycotts, sit-ins, and freedom rides designed to end legal racial segregation began in the South. These efforts on behalf of black rights suggested to sympathetic historians that studying the abolitionists could provide insight into and support for the freedom struggle, as well as clarifying the causes of the Civil War and (more generally) the effectiveness of radical reform in American society.[27]

Stampp's book, combined with civil rights activism, led a group of liberal historians known as *neoabolitionists* to reject the revisionist and consensus portrait of abolitionism. Neoabolitionists supported and often participated in Martin Luther King Jr.'s nonviolent movement for change. Like King, and like most abolitionists before the 1850s and immediately after the Civil War, neoabolitionists believed only peaceful efforts could bring lasting social change.[28]

Since the 1960s, the overwhelming tendency among historians of the Civil War era has been to emphasize the positive impact of the civil rights movement on the neoabolitionists' view of the abolitionists. But the civil rights–era belief in nonviolence, renewed comprehension of the role of white racism, and awareness of race-based inequality in America had an equally significant negative impact on the neoabolitionist estimation of the character of the abolitionist movement. The first indication of this negative impact emerged during the 1950s, as historians (after generations of neglect) took an interest in the sense of failure expressed by elderly abolitionists after the Civil War. In 1959, Merton L. Dillon, professor of history at Ohio State University and perhaps the first neoabolitionist historian, published an article entitled "The Failure of the American Abolitionists." Dillon centered his argument on the abolitionists' goal of equal rights for African Americans and dated to the late 1830s the start of the abolitionists' failure to achieve that goal. In his view, "the work of the abolitionists as moral reformers had practically ended by 1844." During these years, most abolitionists moved from nonviolent moral suasion to independent political action, recognizing the right of the U.S. government to use force. Dillon linked this change to focus on white Northern self-interest.

The trend toward abolitionist political engagement, Dillon believed, increased the likelihood of sectional war based on factors other than moral commitment to black rights. Sounding like the post–Civil War abolitionists, Dillon noted that the war destroyed slavery without creating "a society in which the principles of Christianity [prevailed] . . . in which men of all colors could live together in harmony and equality." Dillon held abolitionists responsible for this. "By failing [after 1840] to maintain its original [moral and nonviolent] position," Dillon asserted, "the antislavery movement abandoned all hope of achieving its original goals of ending racial prejudice and persuading slaveholders to abandon their sin." Force "might end slavery," but it could not "end prejudice."[29]

In 1964, James M. McPherson published *The Struggle for Equality: Abolitionists and the Negro in the Civil War and Reconstruction*. This book remains the only comprehensive study of abolitionists during the Civil War and Reconstruction. McPherson acknowledged the influence of the civil rights movement on his book by dedicating it to "all those who [worked during the 1950s and 1960s] . . . to achieve the abolitionist goal of equal rights." King's march on Washington, sit-ins, freedom rides, confrontation between the North and South, and violence directed against civil rights activists inspired McPherson. He perceived "parallels between the events of [his] times and those of exactly a century earlier." He claimed that what he "witnessed and experienced in the 1960s" led him to investigate what "the civil-rights activists of the Civil War era—the abolitionists," achieved.[30]

Implicit in this approach are the issues of abolitionist impact and relevance. In regard to impact, if the abolitionists achieved their goals of emancipation and equal rights, why was another struggle for equality necessary a century later? In regard to relevance, if such dedicated reformers as the abolitionists failed, what chance had their modern counterparts for success? McPherson in 1964 expressed some optimism on both issues, asserting, first, that while the abolitionists during the 1860s did not "forge or control events," they "achieve[d] most of [their] objectives," and second, that the abolitionists were models for modern civil rights activists.[31]

Yet while McPherson agreed with the abolitionists' dominant view in 1870 that they could look back "with considerable satisfaction . . . upon the achievements of the past decade," he had reservations. Like abolitionists after the Civil War and like Dillon, he concluded that efforts resting on force and expediency could not sustain black rights in the face of white Southern resistance and efforts for sectional reconciliation backed by the U.S. government. He did not fully concur with Dillon's observation that this amounted to the "failure of American abolitionists," however; rather than admit abolitionist failure, he claimed that the "American people" failed because they did not follow abolitionist leadership. That leadership, McPherson asserted, lived on in the civil rights movement. This later movement, he believed, had "a greater chance of permanent success than did its counterpart in the 1860s," precisely because the civil rights movement "built partly on the foundations laid down more than a century ago by the abolitionists." The abolitionists' "spirit," McPherson asserted, "still pervades the struggle for racial justice."[32]

During the dozen years following the publication of *The Struggle for Equality,* three historians wrote book-length studies of American abolitionism: Carleton Mabee's *Black Freedom: The Nonviolent Abolitionists from 1850 through the Civil War* (1970), Dillon's *The Abolitionists: The Growth of a Dissenting Minority* (1974), and James Brewer Stewart's *Holy Warriors: The Abolitionists and American Slavery* (1976). As their titles indicate, these books (unlike McPherson's) did not focus exclusively on the abolitionists during the Civil War and Reconstruction. Instead they looked more broadly at abolitionism into the 1860s and 1870s.

In light of Mabee's use of the phrase "nonviolent abolitionists" in his subtitle, it is not surprising that he, most carefully of the three historians, described the transition in 1861 among some abolitionists from pacifism to support of a war for union and emancipation. Mabee also defined most explicitly black abolitionists as a distinct group, which he contended had less ambivalence toward the use of force than white abolitionists. But all three historians emphasized the abolitionists' united efforts during the Civil War to foster Northern public support for a war for emancipation and equal rights. All three likewise agreed with McPherson—and the abolitionists themselves—that the movement achieved a great deal. In Stewart's words, abolitionists succeeded in pressing the Union to act on "moral conviction, not military expediency." Mabee went so far as to mention an 1883 recollection that Lincoln in 1865 had declared, "I have been only an instrument. The logic and moral powers of Garrison and the antislavery people of the country and the army have done all."[33]

Dillon and Stewart emphasized the abolitionists' campaign for the Thirteenth Amendment, their actions in the South to promote black education and civil rights, their role in creating the Freedmen's Bureau, and their positive impact on Reconstruction. In addition, both historians asserted that abolitionists drew together during the war and became more practical, despite their differences in 1864 over Lincoln's reelection and in 1865 over whether or not to disband the American Anti-Slavery Society. Like McPherson, Dillon and Stewart presented these differences as resulting from an internal debate over whether the abolitionists had completed their work or should continue, not over whether they had succeeded or failed.[34]

Yet Mabee, Dillon, and Stewart were less circumspect than McPherson regarding abolitionist failure. Mabee recognized that some abolitionists had concluded, even as the war began, that they had failed. He noted that after the war many abolitionists "came to sense the [Union] victory was hollow," that "'forcible emancipation' would not last." Mabee agreed with the postwar abolitionists that in neither the North nor South had they prepared "most whites for giving genuine freedom to the Negroes." Dillon observed correctly that, as Northern support for black rights dwindled during Reconstruction, abolitionists blamed themselves for not changing "moral values." Emancipation, in Dillon's opinion, "served only to reinforce the dominion of the ruling order." Stewart went further, claiming that Union armies, African American action, and a Northern desire to destroy slaveholders' political power (rather than abolitionist influence) led to emancipation. Very like the postwar abolitionists, he concluded that "warfare between irreconcilable cultures, not moral suasion . . . intervened between the master and his slave. Consequently, emancipation left America not clothed in righteousness, but reconfirmed in its white supremacism."[35]

Another factor, in addition to reliance on abolitionist second thoughts, shaped Mabee's, Dillon's, and Stewart's analyses of the movement's impact in the 1860s: all three books reflected a liberal pessimism concerning reform that began during the late 1960s. Many liberals feared that the civil rights struggle would end in failure and that other mid-twentieth-century reform movements (including those against the Vietnam War and in support of women's rights) would share that fate. Black violence protesting discrimination contributed to this pessimism, much as antislavery violence had a century earlier. Urban black riots began in the Watts district of Los Angeles during the summer of 1965. Rioting intensified in 1967, with outbreaks in Newark, New Jersey, and Detroit, Michigan. In 1968, the National Advisory Commission on Civil Disorder, headed by Illinois governor Otto Kerner (and known as the Kerner Commission), warned that the nation was moving "toward two societies, one black, one white—separate and unequal."[36]

That same year, George Wallace campaigned as a segregationist candidate for president and Republican Richard Nixon unveiled his "southern strategy." Despite Nixon's declaration that he had a secret plan to end the Vietnam War, the war continued into the 1970s. There were fears that Nixon would violate civil liberties and civil rights. Conservative think tanks proliferated, the religious right organized, and a backlash against the women's movement spread.[37]

Mabee, Dillon, and Stewart's view of the fate of reform efforts in the Civil War era and their perception of reactionary threats during their time reinforced each other. Mabee doubted the United States' ability to deal effectively with social and racial issues, arguing that "in the nineteenth century . . . black-white relations threatened to destroy the nation, and they still do in the twentieth century." He reflected that "history sometimes presents terrible dilemmas for which there are no solutions." Reformers in the 1970s, he observed, could try and could "largely fail, as the abolitionists did before us."[38] Dillon noted that reformist successors to the abolitionists in the late nineteenth century, in the women's rights, temperance, anti-prostitution, and labor movements, had failed to "transform the character of their age." He warned that just as the equal rights "promises of the Civil War era . . . had not been kept," a similar outcome might prevail regarding the promises made in the Civil Rights Act of 1964 and the Voting Rights Act of 1965. Despite the achievements of the civil rights movement, he claimed, "reformers [had] once more . . . reached a dead end." Stewart demonstrated slightly more optimism, expressing hope that even though "urban segregation ha[d] replaced the plantation, . . . modern day reformers might learn from the abolitionists' mistakes."[39]

Pessimistic as they were, Mabee, Dillon, and Stewart sought to understand the abolitionist role in American political events stretching from the 1830s into the 1870s. In their view, while abolitionists had failed to achieve real emancipation and equal rights for blacks, their efforts had had a significant positive impact in several respects. Yet, even as these three scholars wrote, two factors led most historians of American abolitionism to conclude that abolitionists had failed much more profoundly to influence the major events of their time.

The first factor resulted from a neoabolitionist attempt to refute revisionist and consensus portrayals of abolitionists as irrational fanatics who pushed the United States into a needless civil war. Four decades before Mabee, Dillon, and Stewart's books appeared, historians Charles and Mary Beard found no place for abolitionist impact on what the Beards regarded as an antebellum class struggle between the "planting aristocracy of the South" and the "capitalists, laborers, and farmers of the North and West." During the 1960s, some neoabolitionists reached a similar conclusion. In defense of abolitionist rationality, these historians portrayed white abolitionists not as radical moralists, but as representatives of a rising entrepreneurial class, who embraced values associated with Northern industrialization. In this view, white abolitionists were motivated not by sympathy for African Americans in slavery but by commitment to wage labor, social mobility, and individualism. Self-interest, not morality, led white abolitionists to condemn the South's traditional values, agricultural economy, and primitive labor system.[40]

The second factor arose from the racial polarization and violence that affected intellectual discourse during the late 1960s. Within this context, neoabolitionists questioned white abolitionists' commitment to racial justice. It seemed that even as white abolitionists decried racial injustice, many of them could not free themselves from prejudice. They failed to achieve true emancipation because most of them were racists. Well into the 1980s, most historians of the antislavery movement contended that white abolitionist racism alienated black abolitionists, frustrated black aspirations, divided the abolition movement, and undermined its objectives.[41]

How could such a limited and conflicted effort have either a positive or negative impact on major events? How could abolitionism have been a factor in causing the Civil War and emancipation? As early as 1965, when historians still regarded abolitionists as radicals, the long-standing view that they had had political influence was already waning among those who studied them. According to the preeminent neoabolitionist historian Martin Duberman, "The abolitionist movement never became a major channel of Northern antislavery sentiment. It remained in 1860 what it had been in 1830: the small but not still voice of radical reform." Four years later, Larry Gara traced the origins of the Republican Party to Northern fear of Southern political dominance, "rather than to any growth of . . . humanitarian consideration for the slave as an oppressed human being."[42]

During the 1970s, historians of the abolitionist movement returned to emphasizing its moral basis, while furthering the perception that it did not seriously influence the sectional conflict. They described immediatism as a surrogate religion or an attempt at social control in the North. As historians grew certain that abolitionists had exerted no positive influence on American social and political development, they turned their studies inward, examining abolitionists narrowly as members of antislavery social clusters, small religious denominations, and tiny ineffective political parties. Rather than center on the abolitionists' impact on American political history and Civil War causation, many historians concentrated on what it meant to an individual to be an abolitionist. Others relied on huge collections of abolitionist writings to explore gender, race, and religion in antebellum Northern society.[43]

In 1979, historian Donald M. Scott wrote, "Immediatism was less a program of what to do about slavery than . . . a 'disposition,' a state of being in which the heart and will were set irrevocably against slavery . . . making immediatism the sign of whether or not a person was a saved Christian." In 1981, Lawrence J. Friedman, who studied abolitionist social clusters, went so far as to contend that "sectional conflict, Civil War, and legal emancipation would probably have occurred even if there had been no active abolition movement."[44]

Since 1981, most historians of the abolitionist movement have continued to explore its inner relationships, its reflection of cultural developments, and it revelations concerning gender and race. For example, Paul Goodman's *Of One Blood: Abolitionism and the Origins of Racial Equality* (1998) analyzes (with little reference to national politics) the development, positive and negative, of white abolitionist attitudes toward African Americans. John Stauffer's *The Black Hearts of Men: Radical Abolitionists and the Transformation of Race* (2002) explores the friendship among four abolitionists, two black and two white, rather than their impact on sectionalism.[45]

Nearly all the essays in *Prophets of Protest: Reconsidering the History of American Abolitionism* (2006), edited by Stauffer and Timothy Patrick McCarthy, likewise ignore abolitionist agency in the sectional struggle. Instead the essayists deal with the impact of black abolitionists on the movement, abolitionist use of photography, the role of the printing press in the movement, and the portrayal of abolitionists in twentieth-century films. On a positive note, essays in *Prophets of Protest* and in Richard M. Newman's *The Transformation of American Abolitionism: Fighting Slavery in the Early Republic* reveal how black abolitionists shaped the entire abolition movement. In doing so, these studies counteract the 1970s interpretation of white abolitionists as driven by a racial prejudice little different from that of other white Northerners.[46]

Most historians of American abolitionism and the Civil War era have nevertheless remained leery of addressing the abolitionist involvement in the Civil War. In *Ballots for Freedom: Antislavery Politics in the United States* (1976), Richard H. Sewell admirably develops the impact of abolitionism on antebellum politics. But the book stops with the election of 1860 and the start of secession. Jonathan H. Earle's *Jacksonian Antislavery and the Politics of Free Soil* (2004) stops six years short of the Civil War. In *Beyond Garrison: Antislavery and Social Reform* (2005), Bruce Laurie deals with Massachusetts political abolitionism, without reference to the war. Edward B. Rugemer's *The Problem of Emancipation: The Caribbean Roots of the American Civil War* (2008), despite its subtitle, avoids analysis of events leading to the war.

James Oakes's *The Radical and the Republican* (2007), a dual political biography of Douglass and Lincoln, does extend into the Civil War years. But Oakes maintains that Lincoln's practical politics, not Douglass's abolitionism, achieved emancipation. Similarly, Oakes's *Freedom National* (2013) argues that the Republican Party's commitment to denationalize slavery had more to do with ending slavery than had organized abolitionism.[47] In *Neither Ballots nor Bullets: Women Abolitionists and the Civil War* (1991), Wendy Hamond Venet concentrates on the Women's National Loyal League. But while she implies that this organization had impact, she also suggests that its radicalism limited its effectiveness. W. Caleb McDaniel's *Problem of Slavery in the Age*

of Democracy: Garrisonian Abolitionists and Transatlantic Reform (2013) concentrates on internal disputes among Garrisonians rather than on their influence on Union war aims. Eric Foner's *The Fiery Trial: Abraham Lincoln and American Slavery* (2010) describes a more profound abolitionist impact on Lincoln's political development and on Northern opinion during the Civil War. But it is especially lamentable that histories of black abolitionists stop short of the war. This is the case with Benjamin Quarles's classic *Black Abolitionists* (1969), R. J. M. Blackett's *Building an Antislavery Wall: Black Americans in the Atlantic Abolitionist Movement, 1830–1860* (1983), and Shirley J. Yee's *Black Women Abolitionists: A Study of Activism* (1992).[48]

What will it take to get more historians of American abolitionism and of the Civil War era to once again regard abolitionists as influential? Perhaps nothing can achieve this, since it is difficult to deny that abolitionist efforts failed (at least for many decades) to establish black rights. Alternatively, it may simply take a willingness to probe more deeply the issues of abolitionist success and failure. It might take more optimism, in our time, concerning the prospects of progressive reform in regard to such issues as world peace, global warming, distribution of wealth, and human trafficking.

It is not difficult to establish that abolitionists (fanatics or not) had an important role in bringing on the Civil War and helped shape Union emancipatory policies during the war. Historians in the early decades of the twenty-first century appear more willing than the neoabolitionists to recognize that violence, as well as nonviolence, can contribute to social progress. At least one recent study suggests that the North pulled its troops out of the defeated South too soon and thereby sold out black rights.[49] But, given the interactive relationship between current issues and interpretations of the past, negative evaluations of recent American military intervention in Afghanistan, Iraq, and Syria may lead historians once again to question abolitionist support for military emancipation during the Civil War.

Similarly, more research into how reform movements contribute to incremental progress might influence how historians portray the abolitionist impact. As is often observed, Congress did not repeal the Fourteenth and Fifteenth Amendments, which the abolitionists helped bring about. While the Supreme Court for decades misinterpreted these amendments, they nevertheless remained in place, allowing NAACP lawyers and sympathetic federal judges to return them to their original meaning during a period stretching from the late 1930s into the 1960s. The civil rights movement led to an improved racial climate, a growing number of elected black officials, and the election of a black U.S. president in 2008. These developments have influenced studies stressing a positive relationship between black and white abolitionists. Yet even more recent developments may cause another shift in how historians portray the abolitionists' long-term success or failure. These developments include new state-level restrictions that disproportionately threaten black voting rights and multiple examples of racial prejudice among white police officers.

1. Ronald G. Walters, *American Reformers, 1815–1860* (New York: Hill and Wang, 1978), 213. Daniel Walker Howe places these themes in a wider American context. See Howe, *What Hath God Wrought: The Transformation of America, 1851–1848* (New York: Oxford Univ. Press, 2007).

2. *The Liberator* (newspaper, Boston), Dec. 14, 1833; Lewis Perry, *Radical Abolitionism: Anarchy and the Government of God in Antislavery Thought* (1973; reprint, Knoxville: Univ. of Tennessee Press, 1995), 55–91.

3. Stanley Harrold, *The Abolitionists and the South, 1831–1861* (Lexington: Univ. Press of Kentucky, 1995), 64–83; Harrold, *Subversives: Antislavery Community in Washington, D.C., 1828–1865* (Baton Rouge: Louisiana State Univ. Press, 2003), 64–93.

4. Philip S. Foner, ed., *The Life and Writings of Frederick Douglass*, 5 vols. (New York: International, 1972), 1:398–99; Stanley Harrold, *The Rise of Aggressive Abolitionism: Addresses to the Slaves* (Lexington: Univ. Press of Kentucky, 2004), 123–39; [Gerrit Smith], "A Letter to the American Slaves from Those Who Have Fled from American Slavery," in Harrold, *The Rise of Aggressive Abolitionism*, 189–96, quote, 192; Angelina Grimké Weld, qtd. in Gerald Sorin, *Abolitionism: A New Perspective* (New York: Praeger, 1972), 95; Wendell Phillips Garrison and Francis Jackson Garrison, *William Lloyd Garrison, 1805–1879: The Story of His Life Told by His Children*, 4 vols. (New York: Century, 1885–1889), 3:440.

5. Henry C. Wright to William Lloyd Garrison, Jan. 8, 1857, in *Liberator*, Jan. 23, 1857; Perry, *Radical Abolitionism*, 235; Franklin B. Sanborn, ed., *The Life and Letters of John Brown, Liberator of Kansas, and Martyr of Virginia* (1885; reprint, New York: Negro Universities Press, 1969), 131 (3rd quotation).

6. James Oakes argues that Lincoln's and other Republicans' commitment to denationalize slavery by barring it from the territories, ending it in Washington, D.C., and ending the interstate slave trade amounted to a commitment to end slavery in the Southern states. Abolitionists doubted this conclusion. They believed they had to continuously prod Republicans toward immediatism. See Oakes, *Freedom National: The Destruction of Slavery in the United States, 1861–1865* (New York: Norton, 2013), esp. 1–48.

7. Karl Marx and Friedrich Engels, *The Communist Manifesto: A Modern Edition* (New York: Verso, 1998); James M. McPherson, *The Struggle for Equality: Abolitionists and the Negro in the Civil War and Reconstruction*, 1964; 2nd ed. (Princeton, N.J.: Princeton Univ. Press, 1995), 31–37; *Douglass' Monthly* (magazine, Rochester) 3 (Jan. 1861): 388.

8. Henry B. Stanton to Elizabeth Cady Stanton, Apr. [n.d.], 1861, in Elizabeth Cady Stanton Papers, Manuscript Division, Library of Congress (hereafter, LC); Oliver Johnson to J. M. McKim, Apr. 18, 1861, McKim Papers, Cornell University, as quoted in McPherson, *Struggle for Equality*, 48; William Lloyd Garrison to Johnson, Apr. 19, 1861, in Walter M. Merrill and Louis Ruchames, eds., *The Letters of William Lloyd Garrison*, 6 vols. (Cambridge, Mass.: Belknap Press, 1979), 5:17.

9. *Douglass' Monthly* 4 (Aug. 1861): 497–98; *Advocate of Peace*, July–Aug. 1861, May–June 1863, quoted in Carleton Mabee, *Black Freedom: The Nonviolent Abolitionists from 1830 through the Civil War* (New York: Macmillan, 1970), 340.

10. Sarah Grimké to [William Lloyd Garrison], Nov. 30, 1863, in *Proceedings of the American Anti-Slavery Society, at Its Third Decade, held in the City of Philadelphia, Dec. 3d and 4th, 186[3]*

(New York: AASS, 1864), 145; Theodore Weld to Martha Coffin Wright, Mar. 23, 1862 (copy), Garrison Family Papers, Smith Collection, Smith College Library, qtd. in David Hempton, *Evangelical Disenchantment: Nine Portraits of Faith and Doubt* (New Haven, Conn.: Yale Univ. Press, 2008), 85.

11. Elizure Wright to Salmon P. Chase, May 4, 1861, Chase Papers, LC, qtd. in McPherson, *Struggle for Equality*, 61; *Douglass' Monthly* 4 (June 1861): 465–66; *Liberator*, July 12, 1861.

12. Mabee, *Black Freedom*, 337–38; McPherson, *Struggle for Equality*, 9–38, 40–45, 52–93, 116–30, 133–47, 154–91, 221–59, 353–55.

13. Lawrence J. Friedman, *Gregarious Saints: Self and Community in American Abolitionism, 1830–1870* (New York: Cambridge Univ. Press, 1982), 260.

14. AASS, *Proceedings of the American Anti-Slavery Society, at Its Third Decade*, 3, 29–30; W. P. Garrison and F. J. Garrison, *William Lloyd Garrison, 1805–1879*, 4:173.

15. Frederick Douglass to Gentlemen, Apr. 3, 1874, in *Chicago Tribune*, June 11, 1874; Oliver Johnson, *William Lloyd Garrison and His Times* (Boston: Houghton-Mifflin, 1881), 454; James Freeman Clarke, *Anti-Slavery Days: A Sketch of the Struggle which Ended in the Abolition of Slavery in the United States* (New York: R. Worthington, 1884), 222.

16. In a historiographical essay, Richard O. Curry suggests that, for a variety of reasons, abolitionists had a role in causing this failure. See Curry, "The Abolitionists and Reconstruction: A Critical Appraisal," *Journal of Southern History* 34 (Nov. 1968): 527–45.

17. *National Anti-Slavery Standard*, Nov. 23, 1861 (1st quotation); Lydia Maria Child to Gerrit Smith, Jan. 7, 1862, qtd. in Friedman, *Gregarious Saints*, 260 (2nd quotation).

18. AASS, *Proceedings of the American Anti-Slavery Society, at Its Third Decade*, 58, 71, 111–15.

19. *Liberator*, June 2, 1865; Henry C. Wright to Francis and Louisa Hinckley, Nov. 1, 1865, in *Liberator*, Dec. 15, 1865; *National Anti-Slavery Standard* (newspaper, New York and Philadelphia), Nov. 13, 1869; Julie Roy Jeffrey, *Abolitionists Remember: Antislavery Autobiographies and the Unfinished Work of Emancipation* (Chapel Hill: Univ. of North Carolina Press, 2008), 13; Mabee, *Black Freedom*, 424.

20. Samuel Joseph May, *Some Recollections of Our AntiSlavery Conflict* (1869; reprint, Bedford, Mass.: Applewood Books, 2008), 396; William Lloyd Garrison to Henry Wilson, June 5, 1874, in Merrill and Ruchames, eds., *Letters of William Lloyd Garrison*, 6:328–29; *Chicago Tribune*, June 11, 1876; *The Independent* (magazine), July 6, 1876.

21. Frederick Douglass, *Life and Times of Frederick Douglass* (1884; reprint, Whitefish, Mont.: Kessinger, 2004), 588–89; Cassius Marcellus Clay, *The Life of Cassius Marcellus Clay: Memoirs, Writings, and Speeches*, 2 vols. (Cincinnati, Ohio: J. F. Brennan, 1886), 1:596.

22. David W. Blight, *Race and Reunion: The Civil War in American Memory* (Cambridge, Mass.: Belknap Press, 2001), esp. 357–59; Thomas J. Pressley, *Americans Interpret Their Civil War*, paperback ed. (New York: Free Press, 1962), 176–77; Hugh Tulloch, *The Debate on the American Civil War Era* (New York: Manchester Univ. Press, 1999), 209–13.

23. James Ford Rhodes, *History of the United States from the Compromise of 1850*, 9 vols. (New York: Macmillan, 1892–1928), 1: 62–63; Albert Bushnell Hart, *Slavery and Abolition* (1906; reprint, New York: Haskell House, 1968); James G. Randall, *The Civil War and Reconstruction* (Boston, Mass.: D. C. Heath, 1937), 146; McPherson, *Struggle for Equality*, xi; Gilbert Hobbs Barnes, *The Antislavery Impulse, 1830–1844* (1933; reprint, Gloucester, Mass.: Peter Smith, 1973), 197; Dwight L. Dumond, *Antislavery Origins of the Civil War in the United States* (1939; reprint, Ann Arbor: Univ. of Michigan Press, 1959), 107.

24. Barnes, *Antislavery Impulse,* 197; Dumond, *Antislavery Origins of the Civil War,* 107.

25. Avery O. Craven, *The Coming of the Civil War* (New York: Charles Scribner's Sons, 1942), 124–31, 150.

26. Avery O. Craven, "The South in American History," *Historical Outlook* 21 (Mar. 1930): 106; Frank L. Owsley, "The Fundamental Cause of the Civil War: Egocentric Sectionalism," *Journal of Southern History* 7 (Feb. 1941): 16–18; Randall, *Civil War and Reconstruction,* 146.

27. Kenneth M. Stampp, *The Peculiar Institution: Slavery in the Ante-Bellum South* (New York: Knopf, 1956), 141 (quotation); Howard Zinn, "Abolitionists, Freedom Riders, and the Tactics of Agitation," in *The Zinn Reader: Writings on Disobedience and Democracy* (New York: Seven Stories Press, 1997), 115–43.

28. Don E. Fehrenbacher, review of Tilden G. Edelstein, *Strange Enthusiasm: A Life of Thomas Wentworth Higginson,* and Aileen S. Kraditor, *Means and Ends in American Abolitionism,* in *American Historical Review* 75 (Oct. 1969): 212; Tulloch, *Debate on the American Civil War Era,* 90–91; Howard Zinn, *SNCC: The New Abolitionists,* 2nd ed. (Boston, Mass.: Beach, 1965), iv, 14.

29. Merton L. Dillon, "The Failure of American Abolitionists," *Journal of Southern History* 25 (May 1959): 173–76. See also Hugh Davis, "The Failure of Political Abolitionism," *Connecticut Review* 6 (Apr. 1973): 76–86.

30. McPherson, *Struggle for Equality,* v, ix.

31. Ibid., xiii–xiv.

32. Ibid., 430–32.

33. Mabee, *Black Freedom,* 333–34, 337–39, 345–67, 370; James Brewer Stewart, *Holy Warriors: The Abolitionists and American Slavery* (New York: Hill and Wang, 1976), 186.

34. Merton L. Dillon, *The Abolitionists: The Growth of a Dissenting Minority* (New York: Norton, 1974), 251–52, 257–63; Stewart, *Holy Warriors,* 185, 194–99.

35. Mabee, *Black Freedom,* 334–35, 371–74; Dillon, *Abolitionists,* 264–65; Stewart, *Holy Warriors,* 202.

36. United States, Kerner Commission, *Report of the National Commission on Civil Disorder* (Washington, D.C.: GPO, 1968), 1.

37. Maurice Isserman and Michael Kazin, *America Divided: The Civil War of the 1960s,* 3rd ed. (New York: Oxford Univ. Press, 2007).

38. Mabee, *Black Freedom,* 374, 379.

39. Dillon, *Abolitionists,* 226, 274–75; Stewart, *Holy Warriors,* 203.

40. Charles A. Beard and Mary R. Beard, *The Rise of American Civilization,* 2 vols. (New York: Macmillan, 1927), 1:667, 698–99, 710, 2:51–53; Tolloch, *Debate on the American Civil War,* 90–94; Friedman, *Gregarious Saints,* 236.

41. Jane H. Pease and William H. Pease, "Antislavery Ambivalence: Immediatism, Expediency, Race," *American Quarterly* 17 (Winter 1965): 682–94; Pease and Pease, *They Who Would Be Free: Blacks' Search for Freedom, 1830–1861* (New York: Athenaeum, 1974), 68–94; Merton L. Dillon, "The Abolitionists: A Decade of Historiography, 1959–1969," *Journal of Southern History* 35 (Nov. 1969): 500–22; Eric Foner, "The Causes of the Civil War: Recent Interpretations and New Directions," *Civil War History* 20 (Sept. 1976): 198; Lawrence J. Friedman, "'Historical Topics Sometimes Run Dry': The State of Abolitionist Studies," *Historian* 43 (Feb. 1981): 177–94; Walters, *Antislavery Appeal,* 70–78; James Brewer Stewart, "Young Turks and Old Turkeys: Abolitionists, Historians, and the Aging Process, "*Reviews in American History*

(June 1983): 226–37; James L. Huston, "The Experiential Basis of the Northern Antislavery Impulse," *Journal of Southern History* 56 (Nov. 1990): 609–20.

42. Martin Duberman, "The Northern Response to Slavery," in Martin Duberman, ed., *The Antislavery Vanguard: New Essays on the Abolitionists* (Princeton, N.J.: Princeton Univ. Press, 1965), 395; Larry Gara, "Slavery and the Slave Power: A Crucial Distinction," *Civil War History* 15 (Mar. 1969): 18.

43. McPherson, *Struggle for Equality*, 3; David Brion Davis, "The Emergence of Immediatism in British and American Antislavery Thought," *Mississippi Valley Historical* Review 49 (Sept. 1962): 229; David Brion Davis, "Antislavery or Abolition?" *Reviews in American History* 1 (Mar. 1973): 95–99; Frederick J. Blue, *The Free Soilers: Third Party Politics 1848–54* (Urbana: Univ. of Illinois Press, 1973), 2; Jane H. Pease and William H. Pease, "Ends, Means, and Attitudes: Black-White Conflict in the Antislavery Movement," *Civil War History* 18 (June 1972): 117–28; Blanche Glassman Hersh, "'Am I Not a Woman and a Sister?' Abolilitionist Beginnings of Nineteenth-Century Feminism," in *Antislavery Reconsidered: New Perspectives on the Abolitionists,* ed. Lewis Perry and Michael Fellman (Baton Rouge: Louisiana State Univ. Press, 1979), 239–52; Ronald G. Walters, *The Antislavery Appeal: Abolitionists after 1830* (Baltimore, Md.: Johns Hopkins Univ. Press, 1982), xiii, 60–61, 70–87, 95, 111–28; Lawrence J. Friedman, "'Pious Fellowship' and Modernity: A Psychological Interpretation," in *Crusaders and Compromisers: Essays on the Relationship of the Antislavery Struggle to the Antebellum Party System,* ed. Alan M. Kraut (Westport, Ct.: Greenwood, 1983), 160–95; Nancy Hewett, "The Social Origins of Women's Anti-Slavery Politics in Western New York," in Kraut, *Crusaders and Compromisers,* 205–34.

44. Donald M. Scott, "Abolitionism as a Sacred Vocation," in Perry and Fellman, *Antislavery Reconsidered,* 72; Friedman, "'Historical Topics Sometimes Run Dry,'" 194.

45. Paul Goodman, *Of One Blood: Abolitionism and the Origins of Racial Equality* (Berkeley: Univ. of California Press, 1998); John Stauffer, *The Black Hearts of Men: Radical Abolitionists and the Transformation of Race* (Cambridge, Mass.: Harvard Univ. Press, 2002).

46. Timothy Patrick McCarthy and John Stauffer, eds., *Prophets of Protest: Reconsidering the History of American Abolitionism* (New York: New Press, 2006), 42; Richard S. Newman, *The Transformation of American Abolitionism: Fighting Slavery in the Early Republic* (Chapel Hill: Univ. of North Carolina Press, 2002).

47. Richard H. Sewell, *Ballots for Freedom: Antislavery Politics in the United States* (New York: Oxford Univ. Press, 1976); Jonathan H. Earle, *Jacksonian Antislavery and the Politics of Free Soil* (Chapel Hill: Univ. of North Carolina Press, 2004); Bruce Laurie, *Beyond Garrison: Antislavery and Social Reform* (New York: Cambridge Univ. Press, 2005); Edward B. Rugemer, *The Problem of Emancipation: The Caribbean Roots of the American Civil War* (Baton Rouge: Louisiana State Univ. Press, 2008); James Oakes, *The Radical and the Republican: Frederick Douglass, Abraham Lincoln, and the Triumph of Antislavery Politics* (New York: Norton, 2007); Oakes, *Freedom National.* In addition to Oakes's dual biography of Douglass and Lincoln, among other books that extend studies of abolitionism into the Civil War years are: Friedman, *Gregarious Saints;* John R. McKivigan, *The War against Proslavery Religion: Abolitionism and the Northern Churches, 1830–1865* (Ithaca, N.Y.: Cornell Univ. Press, 1984); Herbert Aptheker, *Abolitionism: A Revolutionary Movement* (Boston, Mass.: Twayne, 1989); Julie Roy Jeffrey, *The Great Silent Army of Abolitionism: Ordinary Women in the Antislavery Movement* (Chapel Hill: Univ. of North Carolina Press, 1998). To various degrees these books question abolitionist impact.

48. Wendy Hamond Venet, *Neither Ballots nor Bullets: Women Abolitionists and the Civil War* (Charlottesville: Univ. of Virginia Press, 1991), 20–35, 38–56, 64–93, 123–49); W. Caleb McDaniel, *Problem of Slavery in the Age of Democracy: Garrisonian Abolitionists and Transatlantic Reform* (Baton Rouge: Louisiana State Univ. Press, 2013); Eric Foner, *The Fiery Trial: Abraham Lincoln and American Slavery* (New York: Norton, 2010), 24–29, 180–81, 189–90; Benjamin Quarles, *Black Abolitionists* (New York: Oxford Univ. Press, 1969); R. J. M. Blackett, *Building an Antislavery Wall: Black Americans in the Atlantic Abolitionist Movement 1830–1860* (Baton Rouge: Louisiana State Univ. Press, 1983); Shirley J. Yee, *Black Women Abolitionists: A Study of Activism* (Knoxville: Univ. of Tennessee Press, 1992).

49. Gregory F. Downs, *After Appomattox: Military Occupation and the End of the Civil War* (Cambridge, Mass.: Harvard Univ. Press, 2015).

"As firmly linked to 'Africanus' as was that of the celebrated Scipio"

Abraham Lincoln, Emancipation, and the U.S. Colored Troops

John David Smith

During the first eighteen months of the Civil War, President Abraham Lincoln walked a metaphorical tightrope in his treatment of African Americans generally and of the institution of slavery in particular. To be sure, Lincoln subscribed to the racist stereotypes common to most educated whites of his class and time. He believed that physical differences existed between whites and blacks and that humankind fell into distinct physiological types endowed with certain aptitudes in lesser or greater amounts. Although convinced of Negro inferiority, the president believed that blacks were part of the human family and ideally should be free. Lincoln held a deep belief that all men, regardless of race, shared the desire and the capacity for self-government. He became the first president in American history to discuss emancipation publicly and then even to hint that people of color should be granted limited suffrage.

Lincoln, however, was unquestionably a man of his time and place—not a product of the twentieth-century civil rights movement and twenty-first-century notions of justice and humanity. He almost certainly never envisioned an African American president. Lincoln frequently made racist remarks and jokes. In 1864, for example, when a delegation from Philadelphia's Committee for Recruiting Colored Troops lobbied him to equalize the pay of white and black laborers, the president reportedly replied, smiling: "Well, gentlemen, you wish the pay of 'Cuffie' raised." When Henry Samuel, one of the visitors, objected to his use of the term *Cuffie*, Lincoln, obviously embarrassed, apologized. He blamed the gaffe on his Southern roots and his understanding that in the South "that term is applied without any idea of an offensive nature. I will, however, at the earliest possible moment do all in my power to accede to your request." A month later, the War Department equalized the pay for black and white teamsters.[1]

Lincoln certainly was inconsistent in his antislavery views, and critics, especially those quick to label Lincoln a "racist" beyond the context of his day, often pounce upon such comments. But he possessed strong antislavery credentials, a deep faith in human progress, and, as historian Benjamin Quarles writes, a "natural tendency to sympathize with the slaves."[2] Lincoln judged slavery "a moral wrong and a social evil" and "hoped that the South would eventually take steps to end it voluntarily and peacefully." It was a cancer that had to be cured before it destroyed the body politic.[3] Although mindful and respectful theoretically of the Constitution's protections of African American slavery, Lincoln never wavered from considering the aptly named "peculiar institution" a moral abomination and an anachronistic, premodern labor system.

Lincoln had condemned slavery throughout his political career—in the Illinois Assembly, in the U.S. House of Representatives, and in his famous debates with Stephen A. Douglas. "You know I dislike slavery," he reminded his Kentucky friend Joshua Speed in 1855, adding, "I confess I hate to see the poor creatures hunted down, and caught, and carried back to their stripes, and unrewarded toils." Lincoln went on to explain that "as a nation, we begin by declaring that '*all men are created equal.*' We now practically read it 'all men are created equal, *except* negroes.'" He feared that "when the Know-Nothings get control, it will read 'all men are created equal, except negroes, *and foreigners, and catholics.*' When it comes to this I should prefer emigrating to some country where they make no pretence of loving liberty—to Russia, for instance, where despotism can be taken pure, and without the base alloy of hypocracy [*sic*]."[4] In July 1858 in Chicago, Lincoln urged Illinois voters to "discard all this quibbling about this man and the other man—this race and that race and the other race being inferior, and therefore they must be placed in an inferior position."[5] In his last debate with Douglas in Alton, Illinois, Lincoln noted that such "race" talk was simply a way to deny the promise of equal opportunity from being dispersed "to all people, of all colors, everywhere."[6]

Though opposed to slavery as an inhumane, inefficient labor system and confident that it must eventually disappear, Lincoln nonetheless respected slaveholders' rights under the Constitution and vowed to protect them. As a hardscrabble politician, he understood the complex mechanics and realities of political compromise and social change. Until 1862, Lincoln, like many moderate Republicans, largely put his political faith in containing slavery's extension into the Federal territories and thereby eradicating it in the South. Lincoln thus was no abolitionist but rather, as historian Sean Wilentz suggests, an "anti-slavery non-abolitionist."[7] He considered the abolitionists' program too extreme and unrealistic. Yet many white Southerners judged Lincoln's constitutionalist antislavery views, most notably his opposition to the extension of slavery, too radical.[8] Like his abolitionist supporters, however, Lincoln understood well what historian Joseph A. Glatthaar terms "the contradiction of opposing the institution of slavery yet fighting a war to preserve a union with slaveholders and to defend a constitution that protected slavery in the states."[9] The American Studies scholar Richard Slotkin describes Lincoln's dilemma somewhat differently, as constituting "the underlying problem of race in America—the contradiction between a political state based on the presumption of civic equality and a culture deeply imbued with the values of White supremacy."[10]

Once war began in April 1861, Lincoln sought to reunite the nation, as he later famously informed editor Horace Greeley, with or without slavery.[11] Lincoln struggled with this dialectic for the first year and a half of his presidency. Before 1863, he prioritized preserving the Union over ending black slavery. In mid-1862, however, after months of trying to suppress the Confederates' rebellion by conventional military means, Lincoln began shaping a radical political and military strategy to hit the insurgents where they were most vulnerable. This strategy culminated in the final Emancipation Proclamation.

In its preliminary version, issued on September 22, 1862, Lincoln essentially warned the Confederates that if they did not cease their insurgency by January 1, 1863, he would declare their slaves free. Perhaps Lincoln realized that whether or not he mandated it, as historian William C. Davis writes, the enlistment of black troops would become "the inevitable concomitant of emancipation."[12] Nonetheless, the preliminary document made no mention of arming blacks but instead quoted at length from two congressional acts. The first was an article of war adopted on March 13, 1862, which prohibited members of the U.S. armed forces from returning to slavery thousands of fugitive slaves who entered Union lines; the second was what historians term the Second Confiscation Act, passed on July 17, 1862, which freed the slaves of rebels or those aiding the rebels and prohibited the return of escaped slaves unless their owners could prove their loyalty to the United States. With these two acts Congress had taken a major step forward toward the freeing and arming of slaves—military emancipation. Historian John Hope Franklin believed that Lincoln's issuance of the preliminary Emancipation Proclamation in September did in fact signal the president's acceptance of Negro soldiers in the Union Army.[13] In reality, the military recruitment provision in the final Emancipation Proclamation of January 1863 simply reaffirmed the Militia Act, also passed on July 17, 1862, and the Second Confiscation Act. With these acts, the president accepted blacks into the Federal army—if, how, and when he saw fit. "From a distant perspective," historian J. Matthew Gallman observes, "the flow of events followed an internal logic that seems to make some sense. We can see the seeds of Lincoln's grand proclamation in his earlier words. The political and military events that gradually turned the Union army into an army of liberation, aided by the actions of both white military leaders and runaway slaves, do seem to lead to the Emancipation Proclamation as the predictable next step."[14]

The path to military emancipation in 1863 was anything but direct, however. Although African Americans had served with General George Washington during the American Revolution and with General Andrew Jackson during the War of 1812, a Federal statute enacted in 1792 and revised three years later barred them from serving in the militia and, by tradition, from entering the regular army. Responding to the Fugitive Slave Act of 1850, Northern free blacks vowed to protect themselves by forming militia companies, including the Massasoit Guard in Massachusetts and the Attucks Guards in Ohio and in New York.[15] But following secession in 1861, both state and Federal officials rejected offers by African Americans to fight the Confederates. For the first two years of the Civil War, the best free blacks could do was to enter the Union ranks as teamsters, quartermaster cooks, or personal camp servants.

African Americans nevertheless persistently tried to enlist in the Federal army, and during the Civil War almost eighteen thousand blacks joined the integrated U.S. Navy. Even before South Carolina militiamen fired on Fort Sumter in April 1861, Lincoln had an offer from the Reverend Levin Tilmon, pastor of a black Congregational church in New York City, to recruit "colored volunteers." "In the present crisis, and distracted state of country," Tilmon wrote Lincoln on April 8, 1861, he was prepared to supply black troops, "whenever your honor wishes them."[16] Following Lincoln's call a week later for seventy-five thousand militiamen to suppress the slaveholder's rebellion, blacks throughout the North also offered their services as soldiers. In Philadelphia, blacks began raising two regiments of volunteers—the "Herculean defenders" and the "Hannibal Guards."[17]

In Boston, an African American declared that should the government allow blacks to fight for the Union, "there was not a man who would not leap for his knapsack and musket and they would make it intolerable for old Virginia."[18] Whites briefly enrolled Pittsburgh's "Zouave Cadets" along with Pennsylvania's 12th Volunteer Infantry, but then authorities summarily mustered them out.[19] In August 1862, seven prominent abolitionists, including Joshua Leavitt, Theodore Tilton, and Henry Ward Beecher, petitioned Lincoln to enlist black New Yorkers as soldiers. In their opinion, "thousands of colored persons" existed in New York State alone "whose attachment to the cause of the Union is as great as our own, and who are anxiously awaiting an opportunity to serve their country on the battle field."[20]

Alfred M. Green, an African American school teacher and activist in Philadelphia, held similar views. Within a week after the Confederates attacked Fort Sumter, Green tried to rally blacks to arm and mobilize to squash the slaveholders' rebellion, but officials in Lincoln's administration, then opposed to arming the blacks, spurned his proposals. Green underscored the blacks' rich African past as an impetus to fight in the present war. In his *Letters and Discussions on the Formation of Colored Regiments* (1862), he reiterated his appeals, explaining that "no nation ever has or ever will be emancipated from slavery, and the result of such a prejudice as we are undergoing in this country, but by the sword, wielded too by their own strong arms." Green admonished his fellow blacks to "grasp the sword" despite the "meanness" of the government toward them. Lincoln's reluctance to free slaves and arm free Negroes, Green said, proved a point: "the necessity of our making ourselves felt as a people."[21]

A range of groups and individuals, including abolitionists and other reformers, likewise urged Lincoln to arm the slaves at once. Weeks after the Confederates attacked Fort Sumter, for example, abolitionist Gerrit Smith predicted that further Southern aggression would transform all Northerners "into radical, uncompromising, slave-arming, slave-freeing Abolitionists." "Unless the war shall be ended very soon," Smith wrote in May 1861, "black regiments will be seen marching Southward." Soon after, an anonymous New Yorker admonished Lincoln to "Strike, in the name of God . . . free the slaves and let them swell the army of freedom, and thus save the lives of our brave men, and prevent the utter bankruptcy of the people, by bringing the war to a speedy and triumphal close."[22]

Lieutenant Robert G. Shaw, a young officer in the 2nd Massachusetts Volunteer Regiment, agreed. Destined to command the 54th Massachusetts Volunteer Regiment to glory in its famous assault on Fort Wagner, South Carolina, Shaw asked: "Isn't it extraordinary that the Government won't make use of the instrument that would finish the war sooner than anything else,—viz. the slaves? . . . What a lick it would be at them [the Confederates], to call on all the blacks in the country to come and enlist in our army! They would probably make a fine army after a little drill, and could certainly be kept under better discipline than our independent Yankees."[23]

Despite such appeals, Lincoln remained unmoved, dismissing free blacks who offered to volunteer. From the war's outbreak, the president had insisted that the conflict was a constitutional struggle to keep the Union intact, not a war to destroy slavery, grant citizenship, or arm blacks. He recognized the political and social implications of emancipation and the use of blacks as armed soldiers. Placing blacks on a constitutional, political, and social par with whites would challenge the nation's racial status quo—white supremacy. It would incite the racial phobias of conservative Republicans and Democrats, including fears of miscegenation and insurrection, and would discourage white enlistment into the Union army. Arming blacks also would upset a crucial population—slaveholders in Union border states—that Lincoln was determined to placate, if not please. The North's 226,000 free blacks had long lived under the specter of discriminatory *de facto* and *de jure* Jim Crow—a term coined in Massachusetts during the Age of Jackson. Most whites considered military service in the American republic a civic duty, an honor, and a responsibility reserved for Caucasian males. And before 1863, as historian Allen C. Guelzo notes, Lincoln was "as dubious about the fighting qualities of the black soldiers as other whites."[24]

From Lincoln's vantage point, mobilizing black troops was a delicate matter, far more a controversial and sensitive policy question than a matter of civic and human rights for people of color. Since the start of the armed rebellion, the president had worried about the possible ill effects that the military employment of African Americans might have on various constituencies. Whites generally, and Union military officers in particular, opposed it on racial grounds. Mobilizing black troops would alienate conservative Unionists in the North, as well as those residing in the pivotal border slaveholding states of Kentucky, Maryland, and Missouri. Kentucky, Lincoln's native state, seemingly kept his constant attention. In March 1862, the president urged the loyal border states to accept compensated emancipation—an offer their representatives refused. (In 1861 he also had unsuccessfully proffered compensated emancipation to Delaware slaveholders.) Lincoln believed that emancipation most likely would drive slaveholders in Kentucky out of the Union. He also was uneasy about arming blacks, fearful that such a policy would unify opposition to the Federal government in the Confederate states.[25]

Despite these conservative forces, by the spring of 1862, Lincoln was moving slowly toward the radical step of military emancipation—the twin policy of freeing and arming the slaves and welcoming Northern free blacks into the Federal army. Freedom and slavery might have been compatible in peace, he reasoned, but not in war—especially a war he was not winning. The failure of General George B. McClellan's peninsular campaign of the spring and summer of 1862 forced Lincoln to consider new policies to suppress the slaveholders' rebellion.[26] Devastating losses of white manpower in later battles—at Antietam, Perryville, and Fredericksburg—confirmed the wisdom of the president's decision. So too did the arrival of thousands of escaped Confederate slaves at Union military lines, a reminder not only of black agency and the determination of blacks to free themselves—what historians term the "self-emancipation process"—but the possible utility of using black manpower for the Union cause.

Lincoln's inability to suppress the rebellion during 1861–62 had depressed morale in the North, discouraged Northern whites from replenishing depleted Union regiments, provided ammunition for the president's political opponents, and encouraged England to threaten to formally recognize the Confederacy. Significantly, too, the Confederacy's military successes depended heavily on slave labor: their work in planting and harvesting crops, tending animals, working in factories, hauling war materiel, building fortifications, and repairing roads and railroads freed white men to serve in the Rebel armies. Given the vital need to change the direction of the war, Lincoln concluded by mid-1862 that emancipation and the arming of the blacks were military necessities. "What I do about slavery, and the colored race," Lincoln explained in a famous public letter to editor Horace Greeley, "I do because it helps to save the Union."[27] Over time, he had concluded that the two were one and the same.

Accordingly, after mid-1862 the president and Congress took small but incremental steps to prepare the way for military emancipation, hopeful that white Northerners would accept freeing and arming blacks if those expediencies shortened the war.

Nevertheless, during the last six months of 1862, the president was most careful not to show his hand on the question of black recruitment. According to Wilentz, he let Congress lead while he operated in the shadows "with stealth and indirection . . . always keeping himself immune from political blame in case of failure, waiting until the 'trial balloons' had proved successful and public opinion had matured before enunciating policy in public."[28] The president's critics, then and now, have faulted Lincoln for vacillating at best and for being disingenuous and dishonest at worst in his approach to emancipation. Yet historian Richard Carwardine observes that two factors ultimately motivated Lincoln: "opportunism and idealism." His government needed soldiers. Mobilizing blacks as soldiers would simultaneously prevent ex-slaves from entering the Northern labor market and prepare them for life as freedmen after the cessation of hostilities.[29]

During the last six months of 1862, Lincoln purposely avoided mentioning the arming of blacks. He continued to hope that the Confederates would stop fighting; he feared alienating the loyal border states. When the topic of accepting black soldiers came up, Lincoln made clear his opposition to it. Slyly hesitant, calculating, and, above all, deliberate, Lincoln neither closed doors nor opened them. He was characteristically noncommittal. Yet emancipation and military recruitment were on the threshold. According to Jean H. Baker, Lincoln, second only to Calvin Coolidge, "was our most close-mouthed president."[30] In July 1862, Whitelaw Reid, a *Cincinnati Gazette* journalist, wrote of Lincoln that regarding military emancipation, "[n]ever was a man more cat-like in stealthily feeling his way before him."[31]

In July, for example, Lincoln told his friend Orville Hickman Browning that African Americans would not be armed. Such a policy, he said, would be more harmful than beneficial to the army. Browning, also a native Kentuckian and U.S. senator from Illinois, advised Lincoln that, based on Illinois public opinion, "The time may come for arming the negroes. It is not yet." Following this advice, the president repeatedly spurned offers by Northerners to raise black regiments as he was crafting his monumental emancipation decree. "The Emancipation Proclamation was quite enough to ask conservative Unionists to digest for the moment," writes Carwardine; "with elections in the offing in the fall of 1862, he would not ask them to swallow black enlistments, too."[32] The point, however, is that while plotting his emancipation program, Lincoln most assuredly "kept the possibility of black soldiers in mind."[33] In a cabinet meeting later that month, the president reiterated his opposition to arming blacks, maintaining that such a turn would mobilize opposition against the Federal war effort in the Union slave states, in the Midwest, and in the Federal army. It also would unleash a torrent of general resistance among white Northerners to the idea of social and political equality with blacks.[34]

In August and September 1862, Lincoln continued to voice opposition to arming persons of African descent. Professing to have little confidence in blacks as soldiers, he said enlisting them would risk losing white troops by disaffection. In one instance Lincoln declined the services of two regiments of black troops recruited in Kansas. To accept them into the army, Lincoln feared, would be premature. Explaining his rationale to two influential senators, James Harlan of Iowa and Samuel C. Pomeroy of Kansas, the president remarked that he had decided against mobilizing black troops. He would use blacks as teamsters, cooks, and laborers—in support roles—but not as armed soldiers. Lincoln declared that to accept regiments of armed blacks might provoke the loss of forty thousand white soldiers and could drive some of the border states out of the Union. His mind was made up on the black soldiers question. Only "a direct command from providence" would change it.[35]

For all of his professed opposition to arming slaves and free blacks as soldiers, however, Lincoln had in fact begun the process of mobilizing them months before issuing his preliminary emancipation declaration. Part of Lincoln's genius was his determination to use the power of his office to accomplish things that Congress could not or would not achieve. He would initiate legislation and policies that would free black Americans, arm them in the service of the country, and possibly grant them citizenship. By mid-1862, the war's prolongation had prompted Lincoln to conclude that saving the Union and freeing the slaves were inseparable goals; freeing the slaves and then mobilizing them as soldiers would become the nexus that joined them. To an important extent, over the first eighteen months of the war, Lincoln had been directly and indirectly laying the groundwork for emancipating and militarizing the South's four million slaves. Historian Michael Vorenberg notes that although the president's final Emancipation Proclamation signaled a more aggressive means of suppressing the rebellion, it actually "represented no sea change in his approach to emancipation."[36] Before issuing his preliminary Emancipation Proclamation, Lincoln's emancipation project operated on two levels.

The first level was legislative. Lincoln supported three congressional acts that established the legal framework for freeing and then mobilizing slave soldiers. In the First Confiscation Act (signed into law August 6, 1861), Lincoln's government fashioned a policy to deal with fugitive slaves who sought freedom in Federal camps, as had occurred at Fortress Monroe, Virginia, in May 1861 when General Benjamin F. Butler classified such slaves as "contraband of war." The act authorized the seizure of property, including slaves, used to aid the Confederacy and put them to work in auxiliary military roles. This bill had limitations, applying only to bondsmen used militarily against the Federal government, but it was a significant first step. From the very start of the war slaves were freeing themselves by absconding to Federal lines, and by the fourth month of the conflict, Lincoln's government was refusing to return them to their masters.

The Militia Act and the Second Confiscation Act, both enacted on July 17, 1862, empowered the president to enlist blacks on his terms, both in support roles and as armed combatants. Congressmen envisioned the Militia Act as enabling blacks to work as military laborers, thereby freeing up whites to serve in combat units. It also declared male slaves (and their families) belonging to Rebels to be free if engaged in government service. The Second Confiscation Act was more evocative and had greater scope. It declared "forever free" Confederate-owned slaves who made their way to Federal lines or who resided in Confederate territory that fell to Union armies. The bill forbade Federal officers to return fugitive slaves to Confederate masters. It also granted Lincoln authority to employ "persons of African descent" in any way he considered "necessary and proper for the suppression of this rebellion." Finally, it requested that Lincoln colonize freedmen willing to resettle "in some tropical country."[37] The Second Confiscation Act constituted the first official authorization by the Federal government for arming ex-slaves. It is significant because, as historian Christian G. Samito explains, "military service had explicit links to citizenship and inclusion as part of the American people."[38]

The second level was pragmatic. Even before framing his preliminary emancipation edict Lincoln *allowed*, but did not *authorize*, the experimental organization of armed black units in Kansas, South Carolina, and Louisiana. This mobilization occurred piecemeal to relieve temporary manpower shortages. Without fanfare, local commanders organized black troops on a fragmented basis in different military theaters while Lincoln generally looked the other way. Not only did these preliminary mobilizations suggest that Lincoln's administration was moving slowly toward a policy of deploying black troops, but they also exhibited the blacks' eagerness to fight for slavery's overthrow. According to historian Dudley Taylor Cornish, Lincoln raised the early units "on a catch-as-catch-can basis with little or no control from Washington."[39]

In May 1862, General James ("Jim") H. Lane, the legendary antislavery guerilla fighter during "Bleeding Kansas," mustered into Union service the First Indian Home Guard, a triracial unit composed of white Kansans, black ex-slaves and free men, and Native Americans. It operated as a Union force in Indian Territory, in present-day Oklahoma. The War Department neither sanctioned nor forbade Lane's actions. In July, the unit tried and failed to capture Indian Territory from Confederate control.[40] That same month, General David Hunter, also acting without explicit permission from Washington, emancipated slaves in the Department of the South and began organizing South Carolina ex-slaves into the 1st South Carolina Volunteers. Although Lincoln had ceremoniously squashed General John C. Frémont's "freelance emancipation" of Missouri slaves in September 1861, he (through Secretary of War Edwin M. Stanton) "may well have tacitly supported or even quietly initiated Hunter's emancipation order, as a ploy to see how far emancipation could now be pushed." Overwhelmed by public outcry against Hunter's emancipation order, Lincoln countermanded it—but without forcing the general to halt his black recruitment activities.[41] Because Stanton refused to pay his recruits, Hunter had to disband all but one company of his South Carolina force. Within weeks, however, the secretary of war reversed course, authorizing General Rufus Saxton, then military governor of Beaufort, South Carolina, to revive Hunter's black recruitment project, allowing him to muster as many as five thousand black volunteers on the Sea Islands. Lincoln obviously was giving multiple mixed messages, shrewdly taking his time to determine his true course of action.[42]

In August 1862, General Lane opened a recruiting office in Leavenworth, Kansas, welcoming recruits of all races while justifying these efforts under the Second Confiscation Act, rather than through authorization from Washington. Lincoln no doubt waited to see how effective Lane's recruitment was and the extent of the political backlash.

Meanwhile, in the fall of 1862, Stanton authorized General Benjamin F. Butler to organize several regiments of free blacks in the Department of the Gulf. The 1st, 2nd, and 3rd Louisiana Native Guard, as well as the 1st Louisiana Heavy Artillery (African Descent), had originally been mustered in 1862 as all-black state militia units for Confederate service. Upon New Orleans's capitulation to Federal forces in April 1862, the *gens de couleur* switched allegiance, offering to fight for the Union.

Significantly, several of the early black units tasted battle before Lincoln's final Emancipation Proclamation went into effect. For example, Lane's 1st Kansas Colored Volunteers engaged the enemy at Island Mound, Missouri, on October 29, 1862, five weeks after Lincoln's preliminary proclamation. And three companies of Saxton's 1st South Carolina Volunteers conducted coastal expeditions in November 1862. By the time that President Lincoln issued his final military emancipation decree on January 1, 1863, then, as many as four thousand blacks had enlisted in Federal units—in Kansas and the Lower South—without the president's explicit approval.[43]

Although authorized by the Second Confiscation Act to free and admit blacks into the army, Lincoln hesitated to do so during the summer of 1862, behavior that Wilentz interprets as a "tactical—that is to say, political—retreat" on the military emancipation front.[44] Focused privately on conceptualizing his forthcoming emancipation decree, Lincoln publicly went out of his way to give the impression that he opposed emancipation and black recruitment. To be sure, he feared losing the support of tens of thousands of men from the loyal slave states, especially Kentucky, to the Confederate army. As historian James Oakes has explained, the other so-called loyal slave states never matched Kentucky's reactionary strain on racial questions. The commonwealth, he writes, was "especially zealous in its determination to thwart emancipation. When slaves from Alabama and Tennessee followed the Union army as it retreated into Kentucky, authorities in that state imprisoned them as runaway slaves. Those who were not claimed by their owners in Alabama and Tennessee were instead sold to new owners in Kentucky. This was an obvious violation of the Second Confiscation Act and the Emancipation Proclamation, and soon enough Lincoln's judge advocate general, Joseph Holt, ruled that the reenslavement of blacks in Kentucky was illegal."[45] Instead of promoting military emancipation, Lincoln encouraged Federal officers to employ fugitive slaves who entered their lines as military laborers.

Lincoln strategically issued his preliminary Emancipation Proclamation on September 22, 1862, following the Battle of Antietam. McClellan's tactical draw against General Robert E. Lee at Sharpsburg, Maryland, provided the breakthrough Lincoln desperately needed. Not only was the timing right, but circumstances had also rendered such action crucial. The war had become a military stalemate and morale was ebbing in the North. England was threatening to recognize President Jefferson Davis's government. Lincoln needed more men to fill depleted Union regiments. After issuing the proclamation, the president waited cautiously to see how the Rebels would respond.

If the Confederates did not cease their resistance to Federal authority by January 1, 1863, Lincoln warned, he would emancipate all slaves then residing in states currently in rebellion. Hoping that the Confederates might surrender, and setting the political stage in the North for emancipation and the recruitment of blacks, Lincoln created a smokescreen, purposely implying that he opposed arming African Americans. In fact, his government had been enlisting blacks in an unsystematic, fragmented way for months. Although many white Northerners and border state Unionists regarded blacks as their social, cultural, and intellectual inferiors, by late 1862 the exigencies of war had forced Lincoln to reverse his stance on emancipation. But he was more than ready to make the move.

"Various pressures," Wilentz explains, including "Stanton's insistence and the successes, in South Carolina and elsewhere, in raising credible black units, made possible the adoption of a policy that Lincoln had been gently experimenting with well before he issued his preliminary edict of emancipation."[46] Lincoln finally showed his cards on January 1, 1863, slipping the black recruitment clause into his final Emancipation Proclamation, seemingly as an afterthought. Unlike the preliminary document, it lacked provisions devoted to the compensation of slaveholders and to the colonization of freed slaves. But it did include a statement welcoming blacks, both free and slave, into the Federal armies.

African Americans at Port Royal, South Carolina, celebrated a "day of Jubilee" on New Year's Day, 1863. Colonel Thomas Wentworth Higginson, a Boston abolitionist, opened his army camp, home of the 1st South Carolina Volunteers, to a large throng of former slaves. Ceremonies that day included a formal reading of Lincoln's final Emancipation Proclamation and the presentation of the unit's regimental colors. Sergeant Prince Rivers and Corporal Thomas Jordan took possession of the flags on behalf of their comrades. Rivers proclaimed that "he would die before surrendering" the regimental flag, "& that he wanted to show it to all the old masters."[47] More than thirteen hundred miles away, in St. Paul, Minnesota, the editor of the pro-Lincoln *Minnesota Staats-Zeitung* predicted on January 10 that the president's new policy of arming African Americans would immediately transform the war into a Union victory. "Already we have won," the journalist wrote, "if not 4 million new Union soldiers, then still many thousands."[48]

Within days of unveiling his final Emancipation Proclamation, the president made clear that he had issued it as a military measure, to keep the Union intact, and that he would not retract it. "After the commencement of hostilities," he informed General John A. McClernand, "I struggled nearly a year and a half to get along without touching the 'institution'; and when finally I conditionally determined to touch it, I gave a hundred days fair notice of my purpose, to all the States and people, within which time they could have turned it wholly aside, by simply again becoming good citizens of the United States. They chose to disregard it, and I made the peremptory proclamation on what appeared to me to be a military necessity. And being made, it must stand."[49]

As Lincoln had predicted, many white Northerners, civilians and soldiers alike, considered his emancipation program insulting, offensive, and threatening. It drove a wedge deep into the heart of American institutionalized racism—white manhood privilege—in the U.S. military in particular and in the larger society generally. In June 1863, the secretary of the navy, Gideon Welles, referred to "an unconquerable prejudice on the part of many whites against black soldiers. But," he added, "all our increased military strength now comes from the negroes."[50] The following month, Philadelphia aristocrat Sidney George Fisher, who supported military emancipation but opposed racial equality, complained that "the abolitionists are trying to make what they can out of the enlistment of Negro soldiers & are likely to cause a reaction & injure their own cause & the real interest of the Negro." He wrote dismissively of Camp William Penn, the black recruitment center established outside Philadelphia, where abolitionist orators lectured to black recruits on "equality for the Negro race, the right of suffrage, &c," concluding "all this is as absurd as it is dangerous."[51]

Lincoln's freeing of Confederate slaves and his arming of them and of Northern free blacks not only challenged white superiority but had political implications as well, opening the door for future racial equality and citizenship. Arming the slaves made emancipation irrevocable, a point that Lincoln emphasized repeatedly after 1863. Not surprisingly, some whites derided, ridiculed, and taunted the men of the U.S. Colored Troops (USCT) at every opportunity. Such actions sometimes led to racially inspired violence, such as the infamous draft riots in New York City in July 1863, in which white mobs targeted innocent working-class blacks, hunting them down and then beating, lynching, mutilating, and drowning them.[52]

White Northerners also vented their racial fears directly on black soldiers. In November 1863, for example, a group of whites mobbed the 2nd USCT in Philadelphia as the regiment boarded troop trains to New York. Other whites pelted the troop cars with stones as the train wound its way northward. In New York State, Governor Horatio Seymour, an opponent of arming blacks, refused to authorize or support black regiments with state funds. He finally relented, allowing the pro-Lincoln Union League to secure permission from Washington and to finance the raising of the 20th USCT, which received its colors in March 1864. Soon after, however, the regiment's organizers reported "that our recruits . . . were abused worse than any negroes had been on the plantations, and they were abused by men who wore the uniform of the Army of the United States."[53]

Throughout their service, the men of the USCT suffered all manner of discrimination, receiving inferior assignments, inadequate medical care, insufficient training and equipment, and insults from white soldiers. Unlike white troops, they had to contend with a Confederate enemy that considered them escaped slaves and that would re-enslave or execute them as insurrectionists upon capture. Conditions for the USCT generally were inferior, separate, and unequal to that provided white troops—an indication of the blacks' second-class status in the opinion of the War Department's bureaucrats. Segregated in civilian life, Lincoln's black troops remained segregated in the U.S. Army and served under white commissioned officers who themselves faced harsh retribution if captured by the Rebels. Black troops rarely received the basic care, equipment, opportunities, recognition, and respect accorded white soldiers. African Americans' military experience thus largely mirrored their status in American society at large. As late as the spring of 1864, the men of the USCT continued to receive lower pay than their white peers. Their wives and children had no assurance of their freedom until March 1865.[54]

Despite these disadvantages, after 1863 fugitive slaves, liberated slaves, and Northern free blacks flooded Federal recruitment offices to enlist. In Kentucky, Tennessee, and other sections of the Ohio and Mississippi river valleys, recruiters forcibly impressed some slaves into the Federal army. Those who volunteered had various motives: to bury slavery, to defeat the Confederates, to prove their manhood, to reunite their families, and to earn full citizenship.

By war's end, the army had raised 178,975 enlisted men for the USCT. The U.S. War Department's Bureau of Colored Troops organized the soldiers in 133 infantry regiments, 4 independent companies, 7 cavalry regiments, 12 regiments of heavy artillery, and 10 batteries of light artillery. Roughly 19 percent of the troops came from the eighteen Northern states, 24 percent from the four Union slave states, and 57 percent from the eleven Confederate states. The 1860 Federal census reported around 750,000 male slaves, most residing in the Rebel states, of arms-bearing age; accordingly, the majority of the men of the USCT were ex-slaves. Historian William A. Dobak maintains that slaves recruited in the South not only bolstered Union armies but also denied the Rebels a sizable workforce of around 80,000 bonded laborers. Overall, 21 percent of the nation's adult male black population between ages eighteen and forty-five joined the USCT, including almost three-quarters of all black men of military age in the free states. Altogether, African Americans accounted for between 9 percent and 12 percent of all Union troops who served in the war. By any calculation, the USCT signified the first systematic, large-scale effort by the U.S. government to arm African Americans to aid in the nation's defense.[55]

Aware early on of the risks involved in arming black troops, Lincoln considered them experimental, "more as auxiliaries and as symbols than as fighters." The president initially defined the USCT as support troops—best suited to manning isolated forts, thereby freeing up white soldiers for combat.[56] Accordingly, many of the black soldiers, a disproportionate number compared to white troops, performed fatigue or menial labor. They constructed entrenchments and fortifications, garrisoned defensive posts, and loaded and unloaded supplies. Many guarded the invading Union Army's constantly lengthening military railroad and supply lines along the Mississippi River, in Alabama, and across the South Carolina and Florida coasts.

This is not meant to suggest, however, that Lincoln failed to recognize the strategic and symbolic importance of mobilizing the USCT. In April 1863, he informed General Hunter that the black troops engaged in operations in Jacksonville, Florida, mattered a great deal to the Union war effort. "I see the enemy are driving at them [the 1st and 2nd South Carolina Volunteers] fiercely, as is to be expected," Lincoln observed, continuing, "It is important to the enemy that such a force shall *not* take shape, and grow, and thrive, in the South; and in precisely the same proportion, it is important to us that it *shall.*" Lincoln ordered Hunter to proceed with "utmost caution and vigilance" in supervising the USCT: "The enemy will make extra efforts to destroy them; and we should do the same to preserve and increase them."[57]

During the last two years of the war, the USCT served—and served well—in combat divisions in the Armies of the Cumberland, the James, and the Potomac. Admittedly, however, Union commanders limited the combat of most of the black troops to minor engagements, removed from the major campaigns, and put them under the command of relatively obscure officers. Nonetheless, the USCT fought in 449 separate engagements. They served in every military theater: in the East, in the West, in the Mississippi Valley, and in the Trans-Mississippi. They entered combat as early as October 1862 (the skirmish at Island Mound, Missouri, by the 1st Kansas Colored Volunteers) and continued fighting through May 11–12, 1865 (skirmishes at Palmito Ranch, Texas, involving the 62nd USCT), a month after General Lee surrendered at Appomattox. Sixteen black enlisted men received the Medal of Honor, which the government awarded for the first time in 1863.[58]

Unfortunately, when the black soldiers went into combat, as historian Noah Andre Trudeau explains, "they too often entered the fight saddled with the burden of having to prove themselves worthy to their Caucasian comrades. Any misstep during an engagement, or a slip of discipline that would be forgiven a raw white unit, would be held as proof of a black unit's unreliability, a stain that no amount of blood could wash away." The men of the USCT were always put on their mettle, repeatedly required "to prove anew that they would fight."[59]

In August 1863, soon after black troops had distinguished themselves in bloody combat at Fort Wagner, near Charleston, South Carolina, Lincoln informed a friend that his field commanders, including those unsympathetic to abolitionism, now believed that "the emancipation policy, and the use of colored troops, constitute the heaviest blow yet dealt to the rebellion; and that, at least one of those important successes, could not have been achieved when it was, but for the aid of black soldiers." The president predicted that future blacks would "remember that, with silent tongue, and clenched teeth, and steady eye, and well-poised bayonet, they have helped mankind on to this great consummation." He also anticipated that some future whites, referring to Northern Copperheads, would be "unable to forget that, with malignant heart, and deceitful speech, they have strove to hinder it."[60]

Several months later, in his December 1863 annual message, President Lincoln reflected on the impact of his twin policies of emancipation and black recruitment. He admitted that his project of freeing and arming the slaves, undertaken as military measures in January, "gave to the future a new aspect, about which hope, and fear, and doubt contended in uncertain conflict." That said, Lincoln judged those measures to be a success. Union forces had successfully pushed back Rebel borders. Federal forces controlled the Mississippi River as well as Tennessee and Arkansas. And two loyal slave states—Maryland and Missouri—soon would eliminate slavery.[61]

In his message to Congress, Lincoln made special mention of the success of the USCT. "Of those who were slaves at the beginning of the rebellion," he explained, "fully one hundred thousand are now in the United States military service." Roughly one-half of these men bore arms, Lincoln said, "thus giving the double advantage of taking so much labor from the insurgent cause, and supplying the places which otherwise must be filled with so many white men." Commenting on the military performance of the black troops, Lincoln explained: "So far as tested, it is difficult to say they are not as good soldiers as any. No servile insurrection, or tendency to violence or cruelty, has marked the measures of emancipation and arming the blacks." All in all, Lincoln remarked, war-torn America had reached what he termed "the new reckoning. The crisis which threatened to divide the friends of the Union is past."[62] Mindful of the service of the USCT, Lincoln, in his December 1863 Proclamation of Amnesty and Reconstruction, offered pardons to Rebels willing to swear a loyalty oath to the U.S. Constitution and to respect all laws and presidential proclamations regarding emancipation. But he excluded high-ranking Confederate military and civilian officers from this offer, as well as "all who have engaged in any way in treating colored persons or white persons, in charge of such, otherwise than lawfully as prisoners of war."[63]

A year later, in his December 1864 message to Congress, Lincoln expressed a longing for a swift end to hostilities and reaffirmed his commitment to emancipation. No matter what, the president said, he would "not retract or modify the emancipation proclamation, nor shall I return to slavery any person who is free by the terms of that proclamation, or by any Acts of Congress."[64] Deeply moved by Lincoln's message, Colonel Reuben D. Mussey, the commander of the 100th USCT, wrote the president: "God bless you Abraham Lincoln for these noble words that bring joy to so many thousands of Colored Soldiers and so many hundreds of thousands of women and children; words that would of themselves had you no other claim endear you for all time to all who love Freedom and the Nation."[65]

Looking ahead to the postwar world, Lincoln recognized that the government needed to prepare the men of the USCT for civilian life. The president's administration generally welcomed charitable and religious groups that offered basic literacy training to black troops and humanitarian care for the freed people. Late in the war, J. W. Alford of the American Tract Society explained to Adjutant General Lorenzo Thomas that the men of the USCT desperately required education in order to survive in the postwar South, where they would have "few friends" and would encounter hostile whites "ready to prey upon their ignorance." Similarly, in January 1865, the Reverend Samuel F. Colt of the General Assembly of the Presbyterian Church of the United States sought permission from Lincoln to establish "camp schools" for the "freedmen soldiers." Not only would basic education make them "better soldiers and better men," Colt informed Lincoln, but schooling also would "fit them to become safe and useful members of the community after their military service honorably ceases." The president approved Colt's plan, offering his missionaries rations and quarters.[66] Such humanitarian endeavors prepared the way for the establishment, in March 1865, of the Bureau of Refugees, Freedmen, and Abandoned Lands (the Freedmen's Bureau).

More than anyone, Lincoln considered his Emancipation Proclamation the most important act of his presidency. And although he had justified military emancipation as a war measure, Lincoln clearly understood its moral, political, and racial implications. Often preoccupied with his legacy, the president no doubt assumed that his mobilization of black soldiers would earn him a chapter in American history.[67]

In April 1864, Henry Llewellyn Williams, a scholarly twenty-two-year-old New Yorker, wrote Lincoln, announcing his intention of writing a book, *The Negro as a Soldier*. Williams planned to cover the global history of black troops, starting with

Negro troops in Morocco and Algeria. He explained to Lincoln that in order to conduct research for his book, he would need to travel to Paris, first to consult French libraries and then to conduct interviews. Williams unabashedly asked Lincoln, then mired in the third year of the bloodiest war in American history, for government financial assistance for his research in Paris. He assured the president that "should the book meet your approval," he would dedicate his history of black troops to "your Excellency, whose illustrious name will be transmitted to posterity as firmly linked to 'Africanus' as was that of the celebrated Scipio."[68] While no record exists of any further communication between Williams and Lincoln, by 1864 the president had already played the formative role in launching (though not in writing) what would become the rich history of the USCT. By 1865, his administration had mobilized nearly 180,000 black soldiers into the American military, men who etched their story into American history. The history of what Dudley Taylor Cornish termed Lincoln's "sable arm" occupies an important chapter in the nation's emancipation epic and its long and bitter civil rights struggle.

Notes

1. James G. Randall, *Lincoln and the South* (Baton Rouge: Louisiana State Univ. Press, 1946), 2–3; J. G. Randall and Richard N. Current, *Lincoln the President: Last Full Measure* (New York: Dodd, Mead and Co., 1955), 319–20.

2. Benjamin Quarles, *The Negro in the Civil War* (1953; reprint, Boston: Little, Brown, 1969), 134.

3. James M. McPherson, *How Lincoln Won the War with Metaphors*, The Eighth Annual R. Gerald McMurtry Lecture (Fort Wayne, Ind.: Louis A. Warren Lincoln Library and Museum, 1985), 15–16.

4. Abraham Lincoln to Joshua Speed, Aug. 24, 1855, in Abraham Lincoln, *Collected Works of Abraham Lincoln*, ed. Roy P. Basler, 8 vols. (New Brunswick, N.J.: Rutgers Univ. Press, 1953), 2:323 (hereafter *CW*); emphasis in original.

5. Abraham Lincoln, Speech at Chicago, Illinois, July 10, 1858, in Lincoln, *CW*, 2:501.

6. Abraham Lincoln, Seventh and Last Debate with Stephen A. Douglas at Alton, Ill., Oct. 15, 1858, in Lincoln, *CW*, 3:301.

7. Sean Wilentz, "Who Lincoln Was," *New Republic* 240, no. 12–13 (July 15, 2009): 35.

8. James M. McPherson, foreword to *The Hammer and the Anvil: Frederick Douglass, Abraham Lincoln, and the End of Slavery in America*, by Dwight Jon Zimmerman and Wayne Vansant (New York: Hill and Wang, 2012), ix.

9. Joseph A. Glatthaar, *Forged in Battle: The Civil War Alliance of Black Soldiers and White Officers* (New York: Free Press, 1990), 29.

10. Richard Slotkin, *The Long Road to Antietam: How the Civil War Became a Revolution* (New York: W. W. Norton, 2012), 408.

11. Abraham Lincoln to Horace Greeley, Aug. 22, 1862, in Lincoln, *CW*, 5:388.

12. William C. Davis, *Lincoln's Men: How President Lincoln Became Father to an Army and a Nation* (New York: Free Press, 1999), 105.

13. John Hope Franklin, ed., *Civil War Diary of James T. Ayres: Civil War Recruiter* (Springfield, Ill.: Illinois State Historical Society, 1947), xiv.

14. J. Matthew Gallman, foreword to *African American Faces of the Civil War: An Album,* by Ronald S. Coddington (Baltimore, Md.: Johns Hopkins Univ. Press, 2012), xiii.

15. James Oliver Horton and Lois E. Horton, *"The Man and the Martyr": Abraham Lincoln in African American History and Memory,* 45th Fortenbaugh Memorial Lecture, Gettysburg College (Gettysburg, Pa.: Gettysburg College, 2006), 17–18.

16. Levin Tilmon to Abraham Lincoln, Apr. 8, 1861, Abraham Lincoln Papers, Manuscript Division, Library of Congress (hereafter ALP, LC).

17. Christian G. Samito, *Becoming American under Fire: Irish Americans, African Americans, and the Politics of Citizenship during the Civil War Era* (Ithaca, N.Y.: Cornell Univ. Press, 2009), 35.

18. Glatthaar, *Forged in Battle,* 3.

19. Richard Slotkin, *No Quarter: The Battle of the Crater, 1864* (New York: Random House, 2009), 90.

20. Joshua Leavitt et al., printed petition to Abraham Lincoln, Aug. 1862, ALP, LC.

21. Summary of Prof. Alfred M. Green lecture at Banneker Institute, *New York Weekly Anglo-African,* Mar. 2, 1861; William Dusinberre, *Civil War Issues in Philadelphia, 1856–1865* (Philadelphia: Univ. of Pennsylvania Press, 1965), 161–62.

22. Gerrit Smith, "War Meeting in Peterboro. Speech of Gerrit Smith," Apr. 27, 1861, and "Letter to Rev. Dr. G. C. Beckwith," May 18, 1861, both in *Sermons and Speeches of Gerrit Smith* (New York: Ross and Tousey, 1861), 186, 189, 192, 196; Anonymous, *The War and Slavery; or, Victory Only Through Emancipation* (Boston: R. F. Wallcut, 1861), 8.

23. Robert G. Shaw to Sydney Howard Gay, Aug. 6, 1861, in Robert Gould Shaw, *Blue-Eyed Child of Fortune: The Civil War Letters of Colonel Robert Gould Shaw,* ed. Russell Duncan (Athens: Univ. of Georgia Press, 1992), 123.

24. Allen C. Guelzo, *Fateful Lightning: A New History of the Civil War and Reconstruction* (New York: Oxford Univ. Press, 2012), 381.

25. See William C. Harris, *Lincoln and the Border States: Preserving the Union* (Lawrence: Univ. Press of Kansas, 2011).

26. See Glenn David Brasher, *The Peninsula Campaign and the Necessity of Emancipation: African Americans and the Fight for Freedom* (Chapel Hill: Univ. of North Carolina Press, 2012).

27. Abraham Lincoln to Horace Greeley, Aug. 22, 1862, in Lincoln, *CW,* 5:388–89.

28. Wilentz, "Who Lincoln Was," 38.

29. Richard Carwardine, *Lincoln: A Life of Purpose and Power* (New York: Vintage Books, 2007), 220.

30. Jean H. Baker, review of *Lincoln Legends: Hoaxes and Confabulations Associated with Our Greatest President,* by Edward Steers, *Maryland Historical Magazine* 104 (Spring 2009): 82.

31. Whitelaw Reid, quoted in Michael Burlingame, *Abraham Lincoln: A Life,* 2 vols. (Baltimore, Md.: Johns Hopkins Univ. Press, 2008), 2:465.

32. Carwardine, *Lincoln,* 220.

33. Phillip S. Paludan, "Greeley, Colonization, and a 'Deputation of Negroes,'" in *Lincoln Emancipated: The President and the Politics of Race,* ed. Brian R. Dirck (DeKalb: Northern Illinois Univ. Press, 2007), 40.

34. Burlingame, *Abraham Lincoln*, 2:464.

35. Ibid., 2:465.

36. Michael Vorenberg, *Final Freedom: The Civil War, the Abolition of Slavery, and the Thirteenth Amendment* (Cambridge, UK: Cambridge Univ. Press, 2001), 27.

37. "An Act to amend the Act calling forth the Militia to execute the Laws of the Union, suppress Insurrections, and repel Invasions," July 17, 1862, and "An Act to suppress Insurrection, to punish Treason and Rebellion, to seize and confiscate the Property of Rebels, and for other Purposes," July 17, 1862, in U.S. Congress, *The Statutes at Large, Treaties and Proclamations of the United States of America*, 111 vols. to date (Boston: Little, Brown, 1863–), 12:599, 591, 592. On Lincoln and colonization, see Phillip W. Magness, *Colonization after Emancipation: Lincoln and the Movement for Black Resettlement* (Columbia: Univ. of Missouri Press, 2011); Michael J. Douma and Anders Bo Rasmussen, "The Danish St. Croix Project: Revisiting the Lincoln Colonization Program with Foreign-Language Sources," *American Nineteenth Century History* 15, no. 3 (2014): 311–42; and Michael J. Douma, "The Lincoln Administration's Negotiations to Colonize African Americans in Dutch Suriname," *Civil War History* 61 (June 2015): 111–37.

38. Samito, *Becoming American under Fire*, 40.

39. *Encyclopedia of the Confederacy*, ed. Richard N. Current, 4 vols. (New York: Simon and Schuster, 1993), 1:11, s.v. "African American Troops in the Union Army" (by Dudley Taylor Cornish).

40. Eric Foner, *The Fiery Trial: Abraham Lincoln and American Slavery* (New York: W. W. Norton, 2010), 230.

41. Wilentz, "Who Lincoln Was," 37.

42. John David Smith, *Lincoln and the U.S. Colored Troops* (Carbondale: Southern Illinois Univ. Press, 2013), 13, 15.

43. Ibid., 7, 16; John David Smith, "Let Us All Be Grateful That We Have Colored Troops That Will Fight," in *Black Soldiers in Blue: African American Troops in the Civil War Era*, ed. John David Smith (Chapel Hill: Univ. of North Carolina Press, 2002), 20.

44. Wilentz, "Who Lincoln Was," 37.

45. James Oakes, *Freedom National: The Destruction of Slavery in the United States, 1861–1865* (New York: W. W. Norton, 2013), 423. See also Elizabeth D. Leonard, *Lincoln's Forgotten Ally: Judge Advocate General Joseph Holt of Kentucky* (Chapel Hill: Univ. of North Carolina Press, 2011).

46. Wilentz, "Who Lincoln Was," 38.

47. Allen C. Guelzo, *Lincoln's Emancipation Proclamation: The End of Slavery in America* (New York: Simon and Schuster, 2004), 217.

48. *Minnesota Staats-Zeitung*, Jan. 10, 1863, in Martin W. Öfele, *German-Speaking Officers in the U.S. Colored Troops* (Gainesville: Univ. Press of Florida, 2004), 22.

49. Abraham Lincoln to John A. McClernand, Jan. 8, 1863, in Lincoln, *CW*, 6:48–49.

50. Gideon Welles, June 6, 1863, in *Diary of Gideon Welles: Secretary of the Navy Under Lincoln and Johnson*, ed. Howard K. Beale, 2 vols. (New York: W. W. Norton, 1960), 1:324.

51. Sidney George Fisher, July 8, 1863, in *A Philadelphia Perspective: The Civil War Diary of Sidney George Fisher*, ed. Jonathan W. White (New York: Fordham Univ. Press, 2007), 198.

52. Iver Bernstein, *The New York City Draft Riots; Their Significance for American Society and Politics in the Age of the American Civil War* (New York: Oxford Univ. Press, 1990).

53. Guelzo, *Lincoln's Emancipation Proclamation*, 218.

54. Vorenberg, *Final Freedom*, 82.

55. C. W. Foster to E. D. Townsend, Oct. 20, 1865, and E. D. Townsend to Edwin M. Stanton, Oct. 20, 1866, both in U.S. War Department, *The War of the Rebellion: A Compilation of the Official Records of the Union and Confederate Armies*, 128 vols. (Washington, D.C.: GPO, 1880–1901), ser. 3, vol. 5, pp. 138, 1028; Dudley Taylor Cornish, *The Sable Arm: Negro Troops in the Union Army, 1861–1865* (1956; reprint, New York: W. W. Norton, 1966), 288; Ira Berlin, ed., *Freedom: A Documentary History of Emancipation, 1861–1867*, Series 2, *The Black Military Experience*, ed. Ira Berlin, Joseph P. Reidy, and Leslie S. Rowland (Cambridge, UK: Cambridge Univ. Press, 1982), 12, Table 1; Stephanie McCurry, *Confederate Reckoning: Power and Politics in the Civil War South* (Cambridge, Mass.: Harvard Univ. Press, 2010), 319; William A. Dobak, *Freedom by the Sword: The U.S. Colored Troops, 1862–1867* (Washington, D.C.: Center of Military History, U.S. Army, 2011), 504; Ira Berlin, ed., *Freedom: A Documentary History of Emancipation, 1861–1867*, Series 1, vol. 1, *The Destruction of Slavery*, ed. Ira Berlin et al. (Cambridge, UK: Cambridge Univ. Press, 1985), 37.

56. George S. Burkhardt, *Confederate Rage, Yankee Wrath: No Quarter in the Civil War* (Carbondale: Southern Illinois Univ. Press, 2007), 94.

57. Abraham Lincoln to David Hunter, Apr. 1, 1863, in Lincoln, *CW*, 6:158.

58. Noah Andre Trudeau, *Like Men of War: Black Troops in the Civil War, 1862–1865* (Boston: Little, Brown, 1998), 466; Glatthaar, *Forged in Battle*, 71, app. 2.

59. Trudeau, *Like Men of War*, 466.

60. Abraham Lincoln to James C. Conkling, Aug. 26, 1863, in Lincoln, *CW*, 6:409, 410.

61. Abraham Lincoln, Annual Message to Congress, Dec. 8, 1863, in ibid., 7:49–50.

62. Ibid.

63. Abraham Lincoln, Proclamation of Amnesty and Reconstruction, Dec. 8, 1863, in ibid., 7:54–55.

64. Abraham Lincoln, Annual Message to Congress, Dec. 6, 1864, in ibid., 8:152.

65. Reuben D. Mussey to Abraham Lincoln, Dec. 9, 1864, ALP, LC.

66. Keith P. Wilson, *Campfires of Freedom: The Camp Life of Black Soldiers during the Civil War* (Kent, Ohio: Kent State Univ. Press, 2002), 87–88.

67. Foner, *The Fiery Trial*, 240.

68. Henry Llewellyn Williams to Abraham Lincoln, Apr. 26, 1864, ALP, LC.

Reconstructing Other Southerners

The Aftermath of the Civil War in the Cherokee Nation

FAY A. YARBROUGH

In the spring of 2007, the Cherokee Nation of Oklahoma grabbed national, and even international, attention by its March 3 decision to revoke the citizenship rights of about 2,800 Cherokee Freedman who are descended from people owned as slaves by the Cherokee during the nineteenth century.[1] The original slaves had been designated as members of the Cherokee Nation under a U.S.-Cherokee treaty signed in 1866. In 1893, however, the federal Dawes Commission was formed to dissolve tribal governments and end communal tribal ownership of land by the "five civilized tribes"—Cherokee, Choctaw, Chickasaw, Creek, and Seminole—by allotting former tribal lands to individual tribal members.[2] In determining those allotments in the late nineteenth and early twentieth centuries, the commission classified tribal membership in two ways, "by blood" or as "freedmen" (former slaves), listing those so described on separate census rolls. Only those rolls listing tribal members "by blood" included information about Cherokee blood quantum, a concept that traditional Cherokee practice did not recognize.[3] Despite this incongruity, some indigenous groups use these lists or rolls as the basis for determining citizenship today. This policy ignored the fact that some of the individuals placed on the freedmen rolls also had Cherokee ancestry.[4]

In its 2007 vote, by limiting Cherokee citizenship to only those individuals able to trace ancestry to the "by blood" rolls, the Cherokee Nation, in effect, instituted a blood requirement for citizenship. As a part of the campaign to expel descendants of the freedmen, Cherokee member Darren Buzzard circulated an electronic message that warned in part, "FOR OUR DAUGHTER[S] . . . FIGHT AGAINST THE INFILTRATION," a message that invoked the old fear of interracial sex.[5] John Ketcher, another Cherokee who supported the expulsion, claimed that he never saw a black person until he was ten. He was skeptical that the freedmen descendants are part of the Cherokee community and commented, "I think they want some of the goodies that are coming our way."[6] His views no doubt reflect those of many others in the Cherokee Nation. Such responses, and the decision to revoke Cherokee citizenship for freedmen descendents, came, in part, in reaction to the successful legal attempt by Lucy Allen, a descendant of a Cherokee freedman, to obtain voting rights for herself and other freedmen descendants, but they are also part of a much longer legal struggle over the place of freedmen descendants in the Cherokee citizenry, a struggle with roots that go back to the aftermath of the Civil War.

In 1866, the Cherokee Nation stood at a crossroads: by freeing their slaves and including them in the nation's citizenry, Cherokees had to rethink definitions of citizenship and Cherokee identity.[7] The year represented a moment pregnant with possibility. The Cherokees could have chosen to accept their former slaves as full and equal members of society, making race meaningless in discussions of Cherokee citizenship. The Cherokee Nation also could have opted to grant white spouses of Cherokees complete and full rights as Cherokee citizens. Instead, however, the Cherokee Nation chose to uphold and strengthen older racial divisions in Cherokee society and create a hierarchy of legal citizenship. The Cherokees fought against admitting their former slaves into Cherokee citizenship and did so only at the insistence of federal authorities. The Cherokees did finally capitulate to American demands to extend citizenship to the freed slaves, but the Cherokee legislature resolved to keep them separate from Cherokees holding citizenship by blood. Cherokee authorities likewise maintained a separate legal category for whites married to native Cherokees, limiting their legal rights in the Cherokee Nation and admitting them only if they followed specific procedures.

A consideration of the hierarchy of legal citizenship that emerged in the Cherokee Nation after the Civil War reveals several key insights. Initially, Cherokees responded to the destruction of the institution of slavery and the sudden problem of the freedmen by carefully circumscribing the rights of the descendants of slaves in the Cherokee Nation. Among other limits, Cherokee authorities continued to prohibit marriage between Cherokees and the descendants of freedmen. During this same postwar period, however, available marriage records indicate that members of the Cherokee Nation were marrying white Americans with growing frequency. The growing Cherokee acceptance of white marriage partners had very real consequences on Cherokee attitudes toward race and racial hierarchy. The language of legislation and treaties authorized by the Cherokee Nation demonstrates that Cherokees were moving toward a three-tiered understanding of race, reinforced by a hierarchy of legal citizenship. In sum, the post-Emancipation era saw the crystallization of ideas about race in the Cherokee Nation.

Emancipation and the Civil War did little to change the racial attitudes of Cherokees toward blacks or the willingness of the Cherokee Nation to accept marriages between its native citizens and former slaves. While the Cherokee Nation had abolished slavery voluntarily in 1863, it was reluctant to grant citizenship to the freedmen, insisting that they were not entitled to the rights and privileges of Cherokee citizenship. The federal government forced the Cherokee government to accept the former slaves as citizens and grant them rights in Article 9 of the "Treaty with the Cherokee," signed June 19, 1866, which stipulated the inclusion of the ex-slaves into the citizenry: "all freedmen who have been liberated by voluntary act of their former owners or by law, as well as all free colored persons who were in the country at the commencement of the rebellion, and are now residents therein, or who may return within six months, and their descendants, shall have all the rights of native Cherokees."[8]

The Cherokee Nation denied citizenship to those freedmen who returned to the nation after the six-month deadline. Many former slaves missed the deadline because they were unaware of the treaty stipulations. Others did so because they lacked the means to return in the allotted time: during the war, their Cherokee masters had transported them outside the Indian Territory to Texas and Mexico in a quest to preserve the masters' slave property. Still other former slaves claimed to have been detained by Cherokees as they tried to return to the Cherokee Nation. Thus, many freedmen who had lived in the Cherokee Nation as slaves before the war and had legitimate ties to the community failed to obtain Cherokee citizenship.[9]

While the peace concluded with the federal government brought tangible gains to former slaves in the Cherokee Nation, the status of their most intimate relationships proved more ambiguous. Article 4 of the 1866 treaty called for territory in the Canadian District to be reserved for those freedmen who chose to reside there. Articles 5 and 6, meanwhile, permitted inhabitants of this area to establish a local government and a judicial system, in accordance with the laws of the Cherokee Nation, as well as providing for representation in the National Council.[10] Yet, despite the influx of a large number of new black citizens into the nation, the Cherokee legislature made no adjustments to the laws governing interracial marriage or to antiamalgamation statutes.

In the face of Cherokee reluctance to accept the newest citizens of their nation, the U.S. government pushed for equality between freedmen and Cherokees by ordering the U.S. military to treat freedmen as members of the Cherokee Nation, granting them the same annuities, land, and educational advantages given the native Cherokees. Federal authorities even assigned Brevet Major General John B. Sanborn to regulate relations between the freedmen and the Cherokees. The 1866 treaty fundamentally redefined Cherokee citizenship by admitting to the citizenry a population without clan or ancestral ties to the Cherokee Nation. Cherokee society was organized into clans figured by matrilineal descent from a common ancestor; in unions between Cherokees of different clans, any children produced belonged to the mother's clan.[11]

The children of Cherokee women and non-Cherokee men likewise belonged to the mother's clan and therefore had an undeniable claim to membership in the nation.[12] Within the nation, people lacking membership in a clan were not entitled to any individual rights that others were bound to respect. Thus the 1866 treaty challenged the very essence of Cherokee political autonomy: with the United States now making decisions about Cherokee citizenship and mediating the relationship between some of the Cherokee Nation's citizens and its government, the Cherokee Nation's power to determine the legitimacy of members of society diminished.

Although the terms of the 1866 treaty may have admitted some former slaves to Cherokee citizenship, they did not force a change in or reinterpretation of the intermarriage law: the antiamalgamation statute remained on the books.[13] In 1824, the National Council had passed legislation that prohibited intermarriage between African-descended slaves and Indian or white free citizens.[14] In 1839, the council replaced this earlier statute with an act that prohibited intermarriage "between a free male or female citizen with any slave or person of color not entitled to the rights of citizenship under the laws of the Cherokee Nation."[15] However, at the same time that the Cherokee Nation confirmed its prohibition on marriages between Cherokees or whites and people of color, it did repeal laws that proscribed literacy for blacks and barred trading with blacks.[16] The National Council's legal actions suggest that it recognized and was willing to address some of the racial inequities in the law; however, Cherokee lawmakers, like Southern whites, still regarded intermarriage with blacks as taboo.[17] Because of the Civil War, slavery was abolished, and black freedmen, as well as other free people of color, were granted citizenship in the Cherokee Nation, and the argument that the status of blacks made them undesirable marriage partners became moot. Thus, racial or cultural differences alone also could not account for the aversion to intermarriage with blacks; after all, the Cherokees were more than willing to accept intermarriage with whites and had even established detailed procedures to govern the practice. The basis for Cherokee reluctance to allow intermarriage with blacks becomes clearer upon examination of the history of the interactions between blacks and Cherokees, however.

During early contact, Cherokee Indians saw Africans first as the slaves of Europeans and then as fellow bondsmen. As Cherokees came to associate slavery with Africans during this early period, they probably wanted to put as much social distance as possible between themselves and blacks. Cherokee Indians then made a strategic decision to align themselves politically, socially, and economically with whites, even adopting the practice of owning slaves of African descent. In 1835, slaves of African descent constituted 9 percent of the Cherokee population.[18] By 1860, this population had grown to 18 percent.[19] To be sure, the U.S. government pressured the Cherokee Nation to acculturate, but Cherokee elites and lawmakers also embraced some white practices in an effort to ensure the survival and continuance of their nation.

After the Cherokee Nation abolished slavery and could have dealt with blacks more equitably, the Cherokees resisted the further step demanded by the United States, that of admitting blacks to citizenship, granting citizenship to as few blacks as possible and finally taking further action to limit the rights of those freedmen who did obtain citizenship. Despite federal pressure, Cherokee lawmakers attempted to deny full and equal citizenship to blacks, a stance demonstrating that Cherokees did not always blindly accept white attitudes and examples, but tried to act autonomously.

Some scholars blame whites for Cherokee racial attitudes toward blacks. Historian James H. Johnston, for example, contends that "Indians living more nearly in the tribal state and less influenced by the opinions and civilization of the white man welcomed the Negro into the tribes and united freely with them."[20] Similarly, William Loren Katz claims that Europeans promoted racial differences and rivalries between native populations and Africans to push the two groups further apart: "Whites turned Indians into slavehunters and slaveowners and Africans into 'Indian fighters.'"[21] What Johnston and Katz ignore, however, is Cherokee choice and agency—that is, Cherokee complicity with whites in reducing blacks to a position of social inferiority. Cherokees were clearly influenced by white ideas of race and by their observations of how whites treated blacks, both free and slave, but Cherokees also created their own legislation permitting slavery, regulating slave behavior and the activities of free blacks, and prohibiting amalgamation.[22]

The Cherokee Nation, admittedly at the insistence of the United States, accepted black people as citizens, but continued to prohibit marriage with them.[23] This implies that rights to marriage were somehow more sacred or inviolate than rights to citizenship. What made the institution of marriage so exceptional, so deserving of protection? Perhaps it is the nature of the commitment as both religious and secular. Or maybe the simultaneously public and private character of the institution explains its extraordinary status. A more satisfying explanation for the special protections Cherokees gave the institution of marriage is its function as the source of the legitimate members of a society through the production of children.[24] Cherokees had a racial vision of their society that left no room for blacks and attempted to protect Cherokee racial identity by constraining sexual behavior: as Matthew Frye Jacobson comments "The policing of sexual boundaries—the defense against hybridity—is precisely what keeps a racial group a racial group."[25] Blacks and black skin did not fit in with Cherokees' self-perception. Cherokees identified more closely with whites, not just because of physical appearance but also in their perception of the linkage between race and power and success. Whites in the South had held economic, political, and social power over blacks. The South had just lost a war, seemingly about the large population of black slaves residing in the South, while the Northern victors of the war had a very small black population. Blacks appeared to be the least powerful group in the United States, and the Cherokees, by all measures, did not want to imagine themselves as equally impotent or draw any associations or parallels between themselves and blacks.

At precisely the same moment that legislative action maintained the prohibition on marriages between Cherokees and people of African descent, district clerks busily recorded numerous marriages between Cherokees and whites. The National Council passed various laws to govern such unions, but the fullest iteration of the intermarriage law, passed in 1855, required petitions signed by members of the tribe, oaths, testimonials of the worthiness of the potential spouse, and a large fee from white men seeking to marry Cherokee women.[26] An analysis of Cherokee Nation marriage records discloses that legal marriages between Cherokee women and white men increased during the nineteenth century, and also were more frequent than marriages between Cherokee men and white women; both these trends entailed dramatic repercussions for the nation. The inclusion of a growing population of white men fundamentally altered basic principles in Cherokee society. For instance, white husbands wanted to leave property to their offspring, and the federal government pushed Cherokee lawmakers to adjust traditional practices of matrilineal inheritance to permit patrilineal inheritance.[27] Moreover, in response to Cherokee fathers seeking to confer citizenship on their children by white women, Cherokee courts began to accept patrilineal descent in legal claims of Cherokee citizenship.[28] Final evidence of the declining importance of matrilineal descent and the hardening of racial ideology in the Cherokee Nation is the place held in Cherokee society by mixed-race children with Cherokee mothers and black fathers. While traditionally Cherokees would have considered these African-Cherokee children full members of the nation, Cherokee legislators were abridging the rights of such children as early as 1827.[29] Cherokee marriages to whites were giving rise to a growing population of "mixed-race" individuals, a population that was forcing a reconsideration of what it meant to be Cherokee.

The statutory language produced by the Cherokee legislature reflected Cherokee understanding of three distinct racial groups in the nation. In 1866, for instance, the legislature authorized a census stipulating that census officials "take down the name and age of the head of each family, and of each member thereof, of all the citizens of the Cherokee Nation, classing according to age males over eighteen and under eighteen, giving the number of natives, whites, and Africans."[30] Here, lawmakers clearly distinguished native Cherokees from adopted whites and the Cherokee freed people. The actual census results manifest this thinking. The census data merely lists the name of the district, followed by the names of the heads of households. Census takers labeled only the white and colored citizens of the Cherokee Nation, as well as the noncitizen population, such as intruders or those with citizenship claims pending.[31] It is clear, nonetheless, that the first group of citizens listed for each district were "native" Cherokees; the names in this group include many traditional Cherokee names, such as Cher-nee-lucky or Chicken Rooster.[32] Further, census takers listed these individuals first. The native Cherokee population, it would seem, needed no introduction, no special heading, in the minds of census takers.

The official guidelines for conducting the 1880 census include an interesting omission that intimates that Cherokees may have been thinking of themselves more frequently as Indians than as Cherokees: there is no mention of "Cherokees" as a group. The National Council required the enumeration of

> all heads of families, giving a complete registration of births, deaths, and mar-riages, also, the age and sex, and names of all males above the age of eighteen years; the names of all females above the age of eighteen years; the names of all males under the age of eighteen years; the names of all females under the age of eighteen years; the names, sex, and ages of all orphans under sixteen years; the names of all whites entitled by law to citizenship, within the ages above specified; the names of whites not so entitled; the names of all colored persons entitled by law to citizenship, within said ages, the names of all such persons not so entitled; and the names of all Indians not so entitled.[33]

The three groups included for enumeration in the census were whites, colored persons, and Indians. In the case of whites and colored persons, the Council specified that census takers count both those individuals entitled to Cherokee citizenship and those residing in the nation illegally. The provisions regarding the third category for enumeration, Indians, exemplify the change in Cherokee racial self-perception. The early portion of the instructions, specifying the counting of heads of household and the classification of the population by age and gender, did not explicitly men-tion Cherokees or Indians but most likely referred to Cherokees or Cherokees by birth. If the three stated available racial categories were black, white, and Indian, the term *Indian* used later in the instructions must have included the Cherokees. By requiring a separate enumeration from blacks and whites, Cherokees obliquely affirmed their separateness from both groups and their "Indian-ness."

Although the act did not state this explicitly, the separate enumeration of those individuals who would have accessed Cherokee citizenship by adoption or under the treaty of 1866 implies that lawmakers recognized at least two categories of legal citizenship: Cherokee citizens by birth and Cherokee citizens by law. The final seg-ment dealing with counting the human population ordered census officials to name all Indians not entitled to Cherokee citizenship. Where is the directive to count the Indians who were entitled to Cherokee citizenship? After all, as early as 1843, an agreement between the Cherokee, Creek, and Osage Nations permitted the citizens of any of the party nations to become citizens of other party nations.[34] Thus, it is probable that some Creeks or Osages lived in the Cherokee Nation as Cherokee citizens. The language of the act implies that the categories of people entitled to citizenship mentioned earlier included all Indians, so that "Indian" encompassed Cherokees as well as Indians originally from other tribes.

Despite the provisions of the act authorizing the 1880 census, the Cherokee Nation's actual report summarizing the census results includes the language of "blood" and "nativity." Included in the demographic data about the gender and age of Cherokee citizens was an accounting of the number of "Native" and "Adopted" citizens in the nation by district.[35] Cherokees were distinguishing more frequently between Cherokee citizens by birth and by law, a distinction that would not have been made before the nineteenth century. Census takers also collected data on the "Races" of the citizen population. The racial categories named were "Cherokees by blood," "Whites," "Colored," "Delawares," "Shawnees," "Creeks," and "Miscellaneous."[36] The census takers were instructed to note racial categorization but were not asked to divide the Cherokee citizenry by "blood" or "nativity"; nevertheless, the census takers chose to collect and report data in precisely this manner. "Blood" and "nativity" were increasingly important parts of Cherokee identity.

As the Cherokee Nation developed a hierarchy of legal citizenship, those Cherokees who were citizens by birth reaped real economic benefits. Cherokees by birth had civil and political rights, were eligible for all offices in the national government, and received remuneration from annuity funds paid by the federal government for Cherokee land. In addition, because Cherokees owned land communally, Cherokees by birth could improve as much land as they wished, as long as they did not settle and improve land within one-fourth of a mile of another person's field, home, or other improvement. Many noncitizens interpreted this right as access to virtually limitless free land, something landless individuals without funds would have found quite desirable.[37] Cherokees by birth enjoyed the most political rights and freedoms of all citizens in the nation.

Meanwhile, American citizens who married into the Cherokee Nation during the nineteenth century formed another implicit class of Cherokee citizenship, in part because they lacked Cherokee ancestry. Intermarried whites received most civil and political rights but did not receive annuity rights. In other words, through marriages to Cherokee partners, American citizens acquired voting rights in Cherokee elections and gained the right to improve as much of the communally owned public domain as they desired, along with other Cherokee citizens. However, they were not granted the right to receive annuity funds individually, although they could benefit from the annuity funds of their Cherokee spouses. Intermarried white men could not hold high office in the Cherokee Nation or bring suits against other Cherokee citizens in court. Moreover, a white person married to a Cherokee spouse lost Cherokee citizenship if the Cherokee spouse died and the white partner remarried outside the tribe.[38]

Persons of African descent living within the Cherokee Nation fared even less well. Cherokee legislators circumscribed the rights of Cherokee citizens of African descent fairly early, even those who also had Cherokee ancestry. The 1827 constitution of the Cherokee Nation, for example, prohibited any person of "negro or mulatto parentage, either by the father or mother side" from holding any political office in the nation and denied the vote to the children of "Indian men by negro women who may have been set free."[39] On the other hand, the constitution did not bar legal citizens of the nation who were of Cherokee and African descent from improving as much of the communally owned public domain as they desired, but it is unclear if they were eligible for receipt of annuity funds. Before 1866, slaves of African descent, even those also of Cherokee descent, were not citizens at all and possessed no rights. As Cherokee "blood" grew in significance in defining Cherokee citizenship and identity, it became increasingly clear that African "blood" could negate Cherokee "blood."

In 1886, the Cherokee legislature clarified the de facto categories of Cherokee citizenship by grounding them more firmly in legal statutes. On April 27, the National Council passed an act in direct response to the crisis created by admitting freedmen and friendly Indians to Cherokee citizenship. Claiming that the United States had failed to define what rights and privileges were attached to Cherokee citizenship for free colored persons, freedmen, and adopted Indians, the council asserted that it had the sole authority to determine the meaning of the stipulations of the U.S.-Cherokee treaty of 1866. As a consequence, Cherokee lawmakers declared that when "free colored persons, freedmen, and friendly Indians" were granted the rights of native Cherokees, "the phrase 'all the rights of Native Cherokees,' as used in the 9th and 15th Articles of the Treaty of July 19, 1866, between the United States and this Nation, is hereby construed to mean the individual rights, privileges, and benefits enjoyed by white adopted citizens of this Nation."[40] What this meant was that free colored persons, Cherokee freedmen, and friendly Indians all living in the Nation as citizens were entitled to "civil, political, and personal rights," but not to rights to communal Cherokee land ownership or any per capita money, that is, revenue obtained by the Nation through the sale of land.[41] Further, the act acknowledged that adopted whites had not been granted the same rights and privileges as other Cherokee citizens.

At first glance, the act of April 27, 1886, might appear to lump adopted whites, adopted free colored persons, adopted freedmen, and friendly Indians into a single group of equal status; all four groups were granted an inferior class of Cherokee citizenship. Closer examination, however, exposes the real inequities of the law, which placed adopted citizens of African descent in the least tenable position of all adopted citizens. Since white adopted citizens became members of the nation through marriage, they achieved greater access to land than freedmen because of their Cherokee spouses. Cherokee spouses kept their share of revenue from the sale of lands by the nation and could control as much land as their families could improve. Therefore, white adopted citizens generally had indirect access to both per capita money and greater land ownership than that available to free blacks or freedmen. Friendly Indians usually came to agreements with the Cherokee Nation about payments and the occupation of specified territories. Once on designated land, the friendly Indians could distribute land as they saw fit.

Cherokee legislation granted friendly Indians the most favorable class of citizenship available to adopted citizens. Friendly Indians that made treaties with the Cherokee Nation and paid for the right to remain on Cherokee territory could make arrangements with the nation to include rights to the domain and/or per capita money. The Cherokee government's willingness to accord members of other native groups rights that most closely approximated the rights of Cherokees by birth implies recognition of a kind of commonality among indigenous populations. In this case, indigenous groups shared a similar relationship to the land. Further, Cherokee authorities identified groups of friendly Indians as sovereign units capable of maintaining treaty relationships with other sovereign nations. Adopted whites, on the other hand, entered the Cherokee Nation as individuals, with no ability to make treaty agreements. As for the freedmen, the Cherokee Nation likewise did not recognize them as a sovereign unit, even as they joined the Cherokee citizenry in a manner more like that used by the friendly Indians—as a group and through treaty agreement with the federal government—than like that used by adopted whites. Among the differences between freedmen and friendly Indians were that the freedmen did not negotiate any rights themselves and that they lacked the Indians' claim to land as indigenous peoples. More importantly, the Cherokees had opposed the inclusion of their former slaves in the citizenry, acceding to it only at the insistence of the federal government.

The free colored population and freedmen did not have the option of negotiating treaty terms; thus, the act operatively barred them from obtaining per capita money. According to the new 1886 legislation, free colored persons and freedmen could only use land in common with other Cherokee citizens "without acquiring any right or title to the Cherokee domain."[42] They did not become communal owners of the land with native Cherokees which meant that they were not entitled to any proceeds from sales of Cherokee land to the federal government or payments from land usage agreements between Cherokees and other native groups. Article 4 of the 1866 treaty had granted 160 acres to each freed person who chose to live in the designated section of the Cherokee Nation.[43] Native Cherokee citizens and intermarried white citizens, however, could improve as much land as they wanted without acreage restrictions. The freedmen had access to land in the Nation, but not the full access guaranteed to native members of the tribe. Thus, the 1886 law placed greater limits on the citizenship of Cherokee free colored persons and freedmen than any other groups of adopted citizens in the Nation. Cherokees of African descent possessed the bare minimum of rights allowing them to be classified as citizens in the Cherokee Nation. Coupled with the continued refusal of the National Council to recognize marriages between people of color and Indians or whites, the provisions of the April 1886 law further demonstrate the existence of racial prejudice playing out in legislative action and legal statutes.

The language of several treaty agreements between the Cherokee Nation and other indigenous tribes reflects a move toward the official recognition of a common Indian identity among indigenous populations.[44] As early as 1843, the Cherokees, Creeks, and Osages recognized that "the removal of the Indian tribes from the homes of their fathers, east of the Mississippi, has there extinguished our ancient council fires, and changed our position in regard to each other."[45] The compact reflected the tribes' cognizance of their shifting positions on the North American continent and the precarious existence of all indigenous tribes in relation to the U.S. government. The provisions of the agreements ensured amity between the several tribes, granted citizenship to the members of compact nations, and regulated the punishment of criminal activity involving members of the compact nations. Groups that traditionally had considered themselves distinct and separate, and may have even opposed each other in war in the past, were now invoking a shared identity as "Indian tribes."[46]

Later treaties made between the Cherokee Nation and the Delaware and Shawnee tribes in 1867 and 1869 made specific reference to the "Cherokee Nation of Indians," the "Delaware tribe of Indians," and the "Shawnee tribe of Indians."[47] These treaties provided for settling "friendly Indians" on Cherokee lands and sketched out the terms under which "friendly Indians" could receive annuity funds from the federal government. In these examples, tribal names became modifiers of the noun *Indian.* Thus, labels such as *Cherokee, Delaware,* and *Shawnee* described different types of Indians. Members of these different tribes, then, were now perceived as part of a larger group. The Indian authors of the treaty also appeared to differentiate between nations and tribes. The terms *nation* and *tribe* most likely described varying levels of political organization. Nations had more formal governing structures, outlined in a written constitution and specific territorial boundaries. Tribes, on the other hand, were more loosely organized politically, perhaps along more traditional lines, without a written constitution or the institutions of a legislature and courts. The treaties referred to the Cherokees as a nation while referring to the Delaware and Shawnee as tribes, and, indeed, the Cherokees may have had the most formalized and institutionalized government of all of the indigenous groups in North America during the nineteenth century.[48]

The Cherokee Nation simultaneously moved toward creating a common Indian identity and stressing the importance of Cherokee ancestry specifically, contradictory impulses explained by the reality of the relationship between the federal government

and indigenous populations. The U.S. government did not negotiate treaties with Indians generically, but with specific tribal groups. After the Civil War, for instance, federal authorities settled surrender agreements with the Cherokee Nation, the Choctaw and Chickasaw Nations, the Creek Nation, and the Seminole Nation separately, rather than as a unit.[49] These separate agreements and other treaties determined land boundaries, annuity fund payments, and the sale of more territory to the United States. In other words, the treaties were very specific and could include different terms for different populations. Treaties between the United States and the various Indian tribes and nations reified the separate identity of each group. Treaty agreements also recognized the rights of native populations to govern themselves and regulate the behavior of citizens, which served to further reinforce the separation of the Indian nations.

Within the Cherokee Nation, citizens benefited from specific and valuable citizenship rights. The nation possessed finite natural resources in land, timber, and minerals, as well as a fixed supply of money obtained from selling land to the federal government. The Cherokee national government, as well as individual Cherokees, had a vested interest in limiting citizenship because the total population determined the availability of land and the amount of annuity payments to be made to each citizen. The addition of new members through intermarriage or the adoption of freedmen would test the nation's resources. This explains the nineteenth-century Cherokee interest in "blood" or ancestry and its relation to citizenship. In the aftermath of the Civil War, Cherokees considered what it meant to be Cherokee and just who had the right to claim this identity, legally as well as culturally, a debate that continues today.

NOTES

This essay draws from chapter 4 of my book, *Race and the Cherokee Nation: Sovereignty in the Nineteenth Century* (Philadelphia: Univ. of Pennsylvania Press, 2008).

1. "Cherokees Vote to Limit Tribal Membership," *Washington Post*, Mar. 4, 2007, <http://www.washingtonpost.com/wp-dyn/content/article/2007/03/03/AR2007030301705.html>.

2. For more on the allotment process, see Angie Debo, *The Rise and Fall of the Choctaw Republic* (Norman: Univ. of Oklahoma Press, 1934), chs. 11 and 12; Angie Debo, *A History of the Indians of the United States* (Norman: Univ. of Oklahoma Press, 1970), ch. 16; Celia E. Naylor, *African Cherokees in Indian Territory: From Chattel to Citizens* (Chapel Hill: Univ. of North Carolina Press, 2008), chs. 5 and 6; and Circe Sturm, *Blood Politics: Race, Culture, and Identity in the Cherokee Nation of Oklahoma* (Berkeley: Univ. of California Press, 2002), 78–81.

3. For more discussion of blood and blood quantum in the Cherokee Nation, see Fay A. Yarbrough, *Race and the Cherokee Nation: Sovereignty in the Nineteenth Century* (Philadelphia: Univ. of Pennsylvania Press, 2008), 42–43.

4. Naylor, *African Cherokees in Indian Territory*, 179–87.

5. Ellen Knickmeyer, "Cherokee Nation to Vote on Expelling Slaves' Descendants," *Washington Post,* Mar. 3, 2007, <http://www.washingtonpost.com/wp-dyn/content/article /2007/03/02/AR2007030201647.html>. Capital text from the original. Buzzard is a Cherokee citizen and appears as a petitioner to the Supreme Court of the Cherokee Nation. See "Dissenting Opinion of Justice Leeds, SC-06–12," *Cherokee Observer,* Nov./Dec. 2006, <http://www.cherokeeobserver.org/PDF/NovDec06/co111206pg7.pdf>, or, for the full opinion at the Cherokee Nation Judicial Branch website, <http://www.cherokeecourts.org/Portals/73/Documents/ SC-06–12%2014-Dissenting%20Opnion%2012–19–06.pdf>.

6. Adam Geller, "Past and Future Collide in Fight over Cherokee Identity," *USA Today,* Feb. 10, 2007, < http://usatoday30.usatoday.com/news/nation/2007-02-10-cherokeefight_x.htm>.

7. The federal government faced similar questions about citizenship regarding the ex-slave population; for Americans, however, the question of citizenship extended to the native population. Members of Congress grappled with the issue of whether or not native groups should also be granted American citizenship under the Reconstruction amendments. See Joshua Paddison, "Race, Religion, and Naturalization: How the West Shaped Citizenship Debates in the Reconstruction Congress," in *Civil War Wests: Testing the Limits of the United States,* ed. Adam Arenson and Andrew R. Graybill (Berkeley: Univ. of California Press, 2015), 181–201.

8. "Treaty with the Cherokee," June 19, 1866, *Treaties and Agreements of the Five Civilized Tribes,* American Indian Treaties Series (Washington, D.C.: Institute for the Development of Indian Law, 1970–), 60–67: 62 (hereafter, "Treaty with the Cherokee, 1866").

9. Daniel F. Littlefield Jr., *The Cherokee Freedmen: From Emancipation to American Citizenship* (Westport, Conn.: Greenwood Press, 1978), 29.

10. "Treaty with the Cherokee, 1866," 60–67: 60–61.

11. For discussions of matrilineal descent in Cherokee society, see Theda Perdue, *Cherokee Women: Gender and Culture Change, 1700–1835* (Lincoln: Univ. of Nebraska Press, 1998), esp. pp. 81–83 and chs. 1–3; Theda Perdue, *Slavery and the Evolution of Cherokee Society, 1540–1866* (Knoxville: Univ. of Tennessee Press, 1979), 9; John Phillip Reid, *A Law of Blood: The Primitive Law of the Cherokee Nation* (New York: New York Univ. Press, 1970), 113–22; J. Leitch Wright Jr., *The Only Land They Knew: The Tragic Story of the American Indians in the Old South* (New York: Free Press, 1981), 235; Henry Thompson Malone, *Cherokees of the Old South: A People in Transition* (Athens: Univ. of Georgia Press, 1956), 17; Sturm, *Blood Politics,* 28; and Rennard Strickland, *Fire and the Spirits: Cherokee Law from Clan to Court* (Norman: Univ. of Oklahoma Press, 1975), 49–50.

12. Sturm, *Blood Politics,* 31.

13. Littlefield, *Cherokee Freedmen,* 17.

14. *Laws of the Cherokee Nation, 1852: Adopted by the Council at Various Periods* (Tahlequah, Cherokee Nation: Cherokee Advocate Office, 1852), 38 (hereafter, *LCN* 1852).

15. *The Constitution and Laws of the Cherokee Nation: Passed at Tahlequah, Cherokee Nation, 1839–51* (Tahlequah, Cherokee Nation: 1852), 19 (hereafter, *CLCN, 1839–51*).

16. Littlefield, *Cherokee Freedmen,* 16–17.

17. For more on Southern states and the regulation of interracial sex and marriage, see Martha Hodes, ed., *Sex, Love, Race: Crossing Boundaries in North American History* (New York: New York Univ. Press, 1999), esp. the essays by Peter Bardaglio, "'Shamefull Matches': The Regulation of Interracial Sex and Marriage in the South before 1900"; Leslie Dunlap, "The

Reform of Rape Law and the Problem of White Men: Age-of-Consent Campaigns in the South, 1885–1910"; and Peggy Pascoe, "Miscegenation Law, Court Cases, and Ideologies of 'Race' in Twentieth-Century America." See also Mary Frances Berry, "Judging Morality: Sexual Behavior and Legal Consequences in the Late Nineteenth-Century South," *Journal of American History* 78 (Dec. 1991): 835–56; and Andrew D. Weinberger, "A Reappraisal of the Constitutionality of Miscegenation Statutes," *Journal of Negro Education* 26 (Autumn 1957): 435–46.

18. William G. McLoughlin and Walter H. Conser Jr., "The Cherokees in Transition: A Statistical Analysis of the Federal Cherokee Census of 1835," *Journal of American History* 64 (Dec. 1977): 678–703, esp. 686.

19. William Loren Katz, *Black Indians: A Hidden Heritage* (New York: Atheneum, 1986), 135.

20. James Hugo Johnston, *Race Relations in Virginia and Miscegenation in the South, 1776–1860* (Amherst: Univ. of Massachusetts Press, 1970), 284–85.

21. Katz, *Black Indians*, 13.

22. For a broader discussion of the sources and development of white racial ideology, see the following works: Grace Elizabeth Hale, *Making Whiteness: The Culture of Segregation in the South, 1890–1940* (New York: Pantheon Books, 1998) (Hale argues that white Americans created a racial identity for themselves because of the racial ambiguities revealed by the Civil War); Matthew Frye Jacobson, *Whiteness of a Different Color: European Immigrants and the Alchemy of Race* (Cambridge, Mass.: Harvard Univ. Press, 1998) (Jacobson argues that this consciousness of whiteness occurs much sooner); Winthrop Jordan, *White Over Black: American Attitudes Toward the Negro, 1550–1812* (Chapel Hill: Univ. of North Carolina Press, 1968) (Jordan posits that ideas about whiteness and racial difference emerged with the first encounters between Europeans and Africans). See also Kathleen Brown, *Good Wives, Nasty Wenches, and Anxious Patriarchs: Gender, Race, and Power in Colonial Virginia* (Chapel Hill: Univ. of North Carolina Press, 1996), chs. 2, 4, and 6; Alden T. Vaughan, *Roots of American Racism: Essays on the Colonial Experience* (New York: Oxford Univ. Press, 1995) esp. chs. 1, 6, and 7; and Edmund S. Morgan, *American Slavery, American Freedom: The Ordeal of Colonial Virginia* (New York: W. W. Norton, 1975). For further discussion of the debate over which arrived on the American scene first, slavery or racism, see in particular Vaughan's chapter 7; Oscar Handlin and Mary F. Handlin, "Origins of the Southern Labor System," *William and Mary Quarterly* 7 (1950): 199–222; Carl N. Degler, "Slavery and the Genesis of American Race Prejudice," *Comparative Studies in Society and History* 2 (1959): 49–66; and Barbara J. Fields, "Slavery, Race and Ideology in the United States of America," *New Left Review* 181 (May–June 1990): 95–118.

23. It is interesting to note that the United States did not force the Cherokee Nation to modify intermarriage laws and continued to permit laws preventing intermarriage between blacks and whites to remain in state statutes. The federal government was also unwilling to push this issue.

24. Pun intended. It is no accident that the term *legitimacy* also refers to children who are born to parents who are legally married and that rightful heirs to the throne must be legitimate children. In order to hold office in the National Council, one had to have free parents, one of whom must be Cherokee and neither of whom could be of the African race, who "may have been living together as man and wife, according to the customs and laws of this Nation," *Constitution and Laws of the Cherokee Nation, Published by an Act of the National Council 1892*, vol. 10 of *The Constitutions and Laws of the American Indian Tribes* (Parsons, Kans.: Foley R'y Printing Company, 1893), art. 3, secs. 5, 14 (hereafter, *CLCN 1892*. There is

a dual meaning to this term (as opposed to *bastardy* or terms denoting lawfulness) that fits well with discussions of the reproduction of a society.

25. Jacobson, *Whiteness of a Different Color*, 3.

26. *Laws of the Cherokee Nation, Passed During the Years 1839–1867, Compiled by the Authority of the National Council*, vol. 6 of *The Constitutions and Laws of the American Indian Tribes* (St. Louis, Mo.: Missouri Democrat Print, 1868), 104–5 (hereafter, *LCN 1839–1867*).

27. Sarah H. Hill, *Weaving New Worlds: Southeastern Cherokee Women and Their Basketry* (Chapel Hill: Univ. of North Carolina Press, 1997), 95–96; and Sturm, *Blood Politics*, 55.

28. *LCN 1852*, 57. See also Cherokee National Records Microfilm Series (hereafter, CNRMS), roll CHN 73, vol. 1878: 15; see 12–28 for the whole court case.

29. *LCN 1852*, 120.

30. *LCN 1839–1867*, 135–36.

31. *1868–1869 Cherokee Nation Census.* Obtained from Jack Baker of the Cherokee Nation in Oklahoma City, Okla. The census did not have a separate category for those of mixed African and Cherokee descent. Throughout the nineteenth century, this population was increasingly classed with the "colored" population. Cherokees most often considered as Cherokee those individuals of mixed Cherokee and European descent. See Theda Perdue, *Mixed Blood Indians: Racial Construction in the Early South* (Athens: Univ. of Georgia Press, 2003).

32. *1868–1869 Cherokee Nation Census*, 1 and 6. Other examples may be found on pages 17, 18, 19, 30, 36, 42, 51, 67 and passim.

33. *Compiled Laws of the Cherokee Nation, Published by Authority of the National Council*, vol. 9 of *The Constitutions and Laws of the American Indian Tribes* (Tahlequah, Indian Territory: National Advocate Print, 1881), 316–18; see section 3 for the stipulations on who to count. This collection of laws will hereafter be referred to as *CLCN 1881*.

34. *CLCN 1892*, 391–94.

35. *Summary of the census of the Cherokee Nation taken by the authority of the National Council, and in conformity to the constitution, in the year of 1880* (Washington, D.C.: Gibson Brothers, 1881), 6, table A. Hereafter this summary will be referred to as *1880 Cherokee Nation Census*.

36. *1880 Cherokee Nation Census*, 7, table B.

37. *LCN 1852*, 40–41.

38. *LCN 1852*, 118–30; see art. 4, sec. 2 for the limits on office holding. Eligibility for the office of principal chief was restricted to "a natural born citizen"—a provision similar to that applied in the U.S. Constitution to the presidency of the United States. For the restriction placed on intermarried whites seeking to prosecute Cherokees, see *LCN 1839–1867*, 104–5, part 3 on page 105. Part 4 discusses the citizenship status of widowed intermarried whites.

39. For the entire constitution, see *LCN 1852*, 118–301; for the provisions regarding office holding and voting by individuals of African descent, see art. 3, secs. 4 and 7.

40. *CLCN 1892*, 370–71; pages 371–73 contain the entire act. Nancy Hope Sober also mentions this new law in her work *The Intruders: The Illegal Residents of the Cherokee Nation, 1866–1907* (Ponca City, Okla.: Cherokee Books, 1991), 36.

41. *CLCN 1892*, 371–72. Cherokee citizens by birth received annuity funds from the sale of lands owned communally by the tribe. In other words, a citizen by birth had a legal claim to ownership of a portion of communally owned land. Adopted white citizens could improve as much land as they desired, but they were never granted a part in the communal ownership of land and therefore were not entitled to annuity funds. This provision again demonstrates

the efforts of the Cherokee Nation to preserve vital resources, such as land and money, by limiting access.

42. *CLCN 1892*, 372.

43. "Treaty with the Cherokee, 1866," 60–67: 60–61.

44. Reginald Horsman suggests the seeds for a pan-Indian identity may have existed late in the eighteenth century. Though Cherokee mythology described the Cherokees as "the real people," distinct even from other indigenous tribes, Cherokees recognized that "red people regardless of tribal differences were more favored by the Great Spirit." See Horsman, "'The First Man was Red': Cherokee Responses to the Debate over Indian Origins, 1760–1860," *American Quarterly* 41 (June 1989), 243–64: 245.

45. *CLCN 1892*, 391–406 contains several different treaties between the Cherokee Nation and other tribes. For the compact among the several tribes of Indians quoted here, see *CLCN 1892*, 391–97.

46. For instance, the Creeks and Cherokees were not always allies. Gary Nash points out that Indian nations sometimes allied with European powers in opposition to other tribes. See Nash, *Red, White, and Black: The Peoples of Early America*, 4th ed., (Upper Saddle River: Prentice Hall, 2000), 237–38 and ch. 10. James Adair also mentions some of the conflicts between various tribes in *The History of the American Indians* (London: Edward and Charles Dilly, 1775). See especially his accounts of the various nations: "Katahba, Cheerake, Muskohge, Choktah, and Chikkasah," 223–352.

47. *CLCN 1892*, 397–406.

48. The Cherokees did refer to other indigenous groups, such as the Creeks, Osages, and Muskogees, as nations. See *CLCN 1892*, 391–97.

49. See *Treaties and Agreements of the Five Civilized Tribes*, American Indian Treaties Series (Washington, D.C.: Institute for the Development of Indian Law, 1970–), 60–67,131–42, 239–44, and 269–74.

Army of Democracy?

Moving Toward a New History of *Posse Comitatus*

KEVIN ADAMS

In the aftermath of the tragic shootings at Kent State University on May 4, 1970, few commentators spent much time pondering the legal context undergirding the National Guard's deployment to campus.[1] As the emotional reverberations of what *Time* magazine called the "martyrdom that shook the country" resonated throughout American society, the connections between the military and the democratic republic it protected seemed as frayed as they had ever been. Indeed, after the events of the late 1960s, it did not take a pessimist to conclude that democratic values were antithetical to both the military as an institution and the application of state-sanctioned force. As the mother of a participant in the My Lai massacre charged, "I gave them a good boy, and they made him a murderer." Indeed, some veterans of the Vietnam War even joined the chorus: "Yea as I walk through the valley of death," a veteran-poet proclaimed in 1972, "I shall fear no evil / For the valleys are gone / And only death awaits / And I am the evil." It remained an open question whether the military could ever regain its high standing in the eyes of Americans, who, by the early 1970s, did not simply blame the highest levels of civilian and military leadership for unrest at home and abroad, "but apparently harbored not just a lack of confidence in the military, but a deep *distrust* of it."[2]

It had not always been this way. A century before the tragedies of Vietnam and Kent State, a sizable portion of the United States Army was ordered into the streets of ordinary American communities to maintain order. In this instance, however, they arrived under orders distinctly different than the ones guiding the National Guard when it arrived on campuses throughout the United States during the Vietnam War era. With the occupation of the South after the Civil War, the U.S. Army gained many responsibilities, not least of which was its transition into an army of democracy. By protecting the electoral process and by ensuring that citizens—most notably former slaves and their white Republican allies—would enjoy the equal protection of the laws, the extension of certain basic rights, and the benefits of due process, the U.S. Army became an important player in the struggle to remake America. A significant part of this struggle would revolve around the army's ability to serve as auxiliary law enforcement for sheriffs, marshals, and police officials otherwise outgunned and undermanned. Given the Southern context, these duties put the U.S. Army at the forefront of the civil rights struggle after the Civil War. While the doctrine that guided this usage of the army, *posse comitatus,* may strike modern readers as foreign, it had actually served as a bulwark of both federal and state authority since the first days of the republic. So important was it, in fact, that the Democratic Party believed that curtailing the military's *posse comitatus* powers served as an important tool in the counterassault on Reconstruction. As such, *posse comitatus* is an important element not only of Reconstruction, but also of the larger quest to build a more democratic America.

Arriving on American shores via English common law, *posse comitatus* proved an indispensable tool for federal officials from the founding of the United States through the 1870s. It did so, as an expert in the history of American military interventions in civil society reminds us, in "the absence of specific statutory authority."[3] An outgrowth of governmental weakness, *posse comitatus* emerged in medieval England as a tool for local sheriffs seeking to apprehend wrongdoers. Since sheriffs had no permanent body of undersheriffs assisting them, English common law authorized local officials to "enlist the direct aid of civilians in carrying out their enforcement duties."[4] The colonies of British North America continued this practice, as did the newly independent United States, the laws of which allowed federal marshals to call out posses.

In time, however, the American usage of *posse comitatus* came to diverge significantly from medieval English precedent: in the United States, local law enforcement regularly employed federal military forces as the *posse comitatus,* whereas British custom and law held, as The Lord Bathurst put it, "if the Army be sufficient for protecting the people, they must be sufficient for subduing and enslaving the people, as soon as their superiors shall give them a word of command."[5] Even after majoritarian political sentiment shifted in eighteenth-century Britain to permit the existence of a standing army and to countenance use of the military in civil society to maintain order, it is telling that most political elites regarded these developments as "legal unconstitutionalities." The hand-wringing over these issues in Great Britain, however, most ably exposed in the scholarship of John Phillip Reid, had no direct equivalent in the United States.[6] While nothing in federal law prohibited the use of the military in this manner, nothing explicitly allowed it either. It took the uproar over federal enforcement of the Fugitive Slave Act of 1850 in the North for Attorney General Caleb Cushing to lend the semblance of legality to what Americans had been doing for decades. In an official opinion composed in 1854, Cushing wrote, "The posse comitatus comprises every person in the district or county above the age of fifteen years, whatever may be their occupation, whether civilians or not; and including the military of all denominations, militia, soldiers, marines, all of whom are alike bound to obey the commands of the sheriff or marshal. The fact that they are organized as military bodies, under the immediate command of their own officers, does not in any wise affect their legal character. They are still the posse comitatus."[7] From this point on, the "Cushing Doctrine" seemed to sanction federal assistance to law enforcement officials of all stripes. Although observers might wonder at their discipline and organization, federal troops (in practice, it was the army that received the vast majority of *posse comitatus* requests) were nothing more than civilians under arms, even if enlisted men in these detachments came not of their own free will but under orders.[8]

Most nineteenth-century Americans, however, never encountered soldiers fulfilling the function of a *posse comitatus.* Like so many of the army's other duties, its work enforcing domestic law generally took place on the margins of the country, where wide-open spaces and small populations made the army an outsize exemplar of federal authority. In these settings, expansive jurisdictions, a lack of manpower, and small budgets combined with local resistance to all varieties of law enforcement and a fair dose of political corruption to create the perfect environment for disorder. "These realities," Michael Tate remarks, "left only one other legally constituted body with enough manpower and proper mandate to fill the enforcement void—the U.S. Army." Hence, within a generation of American independence, the task of "routinely bolstering civilian law enforcement authorities on the frontier" became one of the U.S. Army's primary missions. Not surprisingly, when given the option, local law enforcement officials called on federal troops frequently, either by directly appealing to the president or by appealing to federal marshals, his statutory proxies. For local officials, relying on federal forces might help deflect the animosity of locals opposed to law-and-order drives, while also allowing them to protect their budgets, since the army would bear the brunt of the expenses. This reality of life in the American West, supplemented by military interventions in labor disputes and anti-Chinese outrages, would persist for the rest of the nineteenth century, even as the larger *posse comitatus* policy underwent serious revision.[9]

While the use of federal forces for law enforcement during the first half of the nineteenth century at times provoked minor controversies, *posse comitatus* only became an object of sustained discussion in the wake of Congressional Reconstruction. Although most contemporary references—including scholarly ones—describe a "Posse Comitatus Act of 1878," such an act does not exist. Instead, what today's commentators misidentify as the "Posse Comitatus Act" actually emerged from the contentious politics of the 45th Congress, which confronted President Rutherford B. Hayes with a Democrat-controlled House of Representatives, and a Republican Senate. Eager to permanently eliminate the possibility of future federal intervention in the states of the former Confederacy, the Democratic House began attaching a series of riders to usually innocuous appropriations bills, riders that sharply constrained federal powers or defunded vital elements of federal enforcement. This attempt by the Democrats to radically reshape federal policy and prerogative through the appropriations process—what Leonard White long ago labeled "coercion by riders"—not only prevented open debate of these significant changes (since Democrats forswore the usual legislative process), but was a tactic they continued to employ throughout the Hayes administration.[10] While most of these attempts were parried by the Republican Senate or Hayes and his veto pen, the Democrats did score some tactical victories. Most important among these was Section 15 of the 1878 Army Appropriations Act, which read:

> From and after the passage of this act it shall not be lawful to employ any part of the Army of the United States, as a posse comitatus, or otherwise, for the purpose of executing the laws, except in such cases and under such circumstances as such employment of said force may be expressly authorized by the Constitution or by act of Congress; and no money appropriated by this act shall be used to pay any of the expenses incurred in the employment of any troops in violation of this section, and any person willfully violating the provisions of this section shall be deemed guilty of a misdemeanor, and on conviction thereof shall be punished by fine not exceeding ten thousand dollars or imprisonment not exceeding two years, or by both such fine and imprisonment.[11]

And with that, a new chapter in the military's long history as an agent of domestic law enforcement had begun.

To this day, the so-called Posse Comitatus Act of 1878 lingers as a minor, albeit exotic, pillar of mainstream American politics. The media environment in which Americans live today is not known for its grasp of nineteenth-century events, yet it is not difficult to find invocations of the "Posse Comitatus Act" in coverage of crises that arguably warrant federal intervention. Following the terrorist attacks of September 11, 2001, the concept briefly garnered attention in the national debate over the Bush administration's counterterrorism proposals. It even served as the title of and the inspiration behind the 2002 finale of *West Wing*, an accomplishment probably unique among nineteenth-century appropriations bills.[12] Shortly thereafter, in the dire aftermath of Hurricane Katrina in 2005, national coverage of the Bush administration's deliberations regarding the proper federal role in the emergency often referenced *posse comitatus*.[13] When it comes to the Civil War era, however, *posse comitatus* was much more than a peculiar remnant of medieval England. On the contrary, it proved absolutely central to the success of Reconstruction on the ground, since using the thousands of federal troops stationed in the South as extremely well-armed and disciplined police officers provided at least some hope of containing disorder enough to permit the remaking of Southern society. It also, contrary to both popular perception and scholarly opinion, remained a viable option for policy makers interested in protecting the rights of African Americans after 1877, thanks to a statutory exception, originating in the 3rd Enforcement Act (1871), purposely inserted into the congressional bill that revised *posse comitatus* policy in 1878.

This finding runs counter to the dominant trends in the historiography of Reconstruction. In fact, some historians regard Congress's decision to revise the United States' traditional approach to *posse comitatus* as one of the nails in the coffin of federal intervention into the South. In his 2009 study of Reconstruction in North Carolina, for example, Mark Bradley makes two erroneous claims: first, that "the army appropriation bill of 1878 . . . prohibited the use of soldiers as a posse under civil officials," and second, that a "Posse Comitatus Act of 1879 made the prohibition permanent." James Hogue's *Uncivil War*, which provides a compelling introduction to the street battles defining the contours of Reconstruction in New Orleans, likewise wrongly insists that Hayes signed an army appropriations bills "forbidding the use of federal troops as a posse comitatus," although this inaccuracy is somewhat counterbalanced by Hogue's recognition of Democrats' continuous efforts to "eviscerate" the army and his discussion of the persistent conflict between Hayes and Democrats in the late 1870s and early 1880s over the meaning of Reconstruction.[14]

More frequently, however, historians working on Reconstruction ignore the subject of *posse comitatus* entirely. For example, not only does Eric Foner fail to mention *posse comitatus* in his magisterial *Reconstruction: America's Unfinished Revolution, 1863–1877*, but its index also neglects to include an entry for the United States Army, the force that implemented Congressional Reconstruction. (It does contain one for the Union Army.) A more recent well-regarded synthesis of the period by Michael Fitzgerald grants more space than Foner to military Reconstruction but still pays no attention to *posse comitatus*.[15] The concept is also absent from William Blair's 2005 article, "The Use of Military Force to Protect the Gains of Reconstruction"; most of the article, in fact, dwells on the military's role in the South before 1870.[16] Finally, Michael Vorenberg's forceful call on historians to reinvigorate the study of Reconstruction by reexamining its legal and constitutional context—matters of crucial importance to any consideration of the military's enforcement of civil rights—bypasses the subject of military intervention altogether.[17]

A few factors seem most responsible for this oversight. First, one consequence of Foner's work has been to root the study of Reconstruction into the society, culture, economy, and politics of the nation as a whole. While this approach has undoubtedly expanded our knowledge of period, it has also tended to marginalize events on the ground in the South, where military interventions were most felt. Second, the traditional tendency of Reconstruction histories to stop their accounts with the Compromise of 1877 leaves outside their purview later congressional battles over the deployment of the military in civil society. Finally, the persistent failure of historians to integrate war and the military into mainstream social, cultural, and political histories of Reconstruction has produced an enormous blank spot on the map of historical knowledge, even though, as one student of the United States Army during Reconstruction points out, "the army was the only agency of the federal government that could have policed the South."[18]

For all this, one would be remiss in ignoring the scholarship produced by historians interested in the Hayes Administration or in Gilded Age politics more broadly. Scholars like Charles Calhoun and Ari Hoogenboom, for example, have understood that the furor over *posse comitatus* early in Hayes's term was but one flank in a heated battle over Reconstruction that continued after the infamous Compromise of 1877. Calhoun's *Conceiving a New Republic* revolves around this conflict, in fact, as various chapters identify in detail the struggle of Republican presidents to protect the gains of Reconstruction. While *Conceiving a New Republic* does not mention *posse comitatus* in its account of the events of 1878, Calhoun emphasizes its importance to the Hayes administration after 1879.[19] Meanwhile, Hoogenboom identifies the *posse comitatus* battle as possessing far-reaching significance for the Democratic campaign to roll back Reconstruction, but his chronology places it in the wrong year. This inaccuracy may stem from Hoogenboom's tendency to follow Hayes's line of thinking that reform in the South could be achieved only through "civil processes—not military force." Nevertheless, Hoogenboom also recognizes Hayes's consistent belief "that federal civil authorities be able to call on the military to suppress violence" during national elections; Hoogenboom's sense of the stakes involved in these battles can be gleaned from his willingness to quote an extended entry from Hayes's diary wherein the president commented, "We are ready to muster out the soldiers, but we dont [*sic*] muster out the flag nor the powers of the law and of the Constitution, which enables us to gain the victory. We dont [*sic*] muster in again the evils that caused the War. Besides it is for the victors to say what shall remain—not for the vanquished."[20]

Even though the scholars cited above display little interest in the military as a historical subject, experts in nineteenth-century military history do exist, even if they are few in number. If one adds to their contingent individuals with an expertise in military law and tracks down work in both genres, one can uncover more detailed discussions of *posse comitatus*.[21] Tellingly, these accounts tend to miss the 3rd Enforcement Act's relationship to statutory exemptions from *posse comitatus* restrictions, to misstate the actual policy, or to emphasize the blanket constraints placed upon the army.

Surprisingly, military historians have handled *posse comitatus* less well than one might expect. What has long been the the standard overview of the army's experiences during Reconstruction, James Sefton's *The United States Army and Reconstruction, 1865–1877,* does not even address the subject, for instance. Meanwhile, those studies that do introduce *posse comitatus* tend to be truncated. For example, Jerry Cooper's classic study, *The Army and Civil Disorder,* notes that while the *posse comitatus* revisions did not eliminate domestic intervention by the army, they had been intended to lessen "the future possibilities of a federal military presence in a political setting." Furthermore, he correctly observes that exceptions to the act existed; his emphasis on industrial disturbances, however, leads him away from the civil rights connection.[22] Robert Wooster's award-winning *The American Military Frontiers* is less useful, since it inaccurately declares that Congress, not the president, controlled the deployment of regulars in civil society. At the same time, his expertise in Western history leads him to recognize that the army continued to exercise its traditional *posse comitatus* role in the midst of chaotic frontier communities.[23] Finally, Michael Tate's *The Frontier Army in the Settlement of the West,* the broadest study of the army's noncombatant roles during the nineteenth century, establishes that while the 1878 Army Appropriations Act "seemed to have closed the door forever on military aid to civilian law enforcement," it actually did nothing of the sort. Tate provides ample evidence that despite "growing public dissatisfaction with the army's continued service as a domestic constabulary," in fact, "most military officers" ignored the "threat of possible legal reprisal," and continued to serve as posses, often at their own discretion. Yet while his account is extremely useful in showing how the dictates of *posse comitatus* were circumvented by army officers in the West, it misses the potential connection to civil rights enforcement, as Tate claims that "the only routine exceptions allowed for the military were protection of Indians, public lands, and international neutrality laws, which were covered by other pieces of legislation."[24]

Early attempts to codify military law into textbook form demonstrate full awareness of *posse comitatus.* Major William Birkhimer's 1892 study, *Military Government and Martial Law,* even contained an entire chapter, "Martial Law in States and Territories," that opened with the declaration that, *posse comitatus* or not, "the President may act within the States independently of State authorities and even against their wishes. There have been numerous instances of this exercise of power in the history of the Government." Yet Birkhimer, joining many of his contemporaries in the Gilded Age in bemoaning the rise of "disorder," declared that "*posse comitatus* has signally failed," because "it was put a stop to by act of June 18, 1878." Arguing that this *posse comitatus* action by Congress had been "based on political considerations alone"—considerations "of doubtful constitutionality"—Birkhimer asserted that it had destroyed an important bulwark of social order. However, nowhere in his account does Birkhimer give a clear and accurate description of the *posse comitatus* clause or its exceptions, leaving readers to wonder why the federal ability to intervene with military force in states and territories is simultaneously imposing and ineffectual.

Thirty-odd years later, in 1925, a monograph from Fort Leavenworth, *Military Aid to the Civil Power*, referred back to the army's original interpretation of the *posse comitatus* restrictions to discover "the occasions when Congress has expressly authorized the use of the federal military forces." However, Cassius Dowell, the JAG officer who wrote the report, was less successful in detailing the statutory exceptions to *posse comitatus.* Although Dowell devoted most of the report to explaining those exceptions relating to insurrection (Revised Statutes 5297, 5298, and 5300), he excluded Revised Statute 5299, an oversight with far-reaching implications.[25]

An important exception to scholars' inability to discern the continued viability of *posse comitatus* interventions (particularly with regard to civil rights enforcement) can be found in two places: a 1941 report on presidential power during civil disturbances issued by the Brookings Institute and Robert Coakley's in-house overview of the military's deployment in domestic disorders.[26] Coakley points out that, far from being diminished, "the president's powers to use both regulars and militias remained undisturbed . . . and by the law of 1861 and the Ku Klux Klan Act they had in fact been substantially strengthened during the Civil War and Reconstruction Era" even after the *posse comitatus* clause entered federal law. Coakley then identifies the salience of civil rights provisions to the statutory exception to the ban on the army's service as a *posse comitatus,* but he deems this fact of little account because "Reconstruction had really come to an end anyway with Hayes' withdrawal of the troops in 1877." Hence, he walks up to the precipice of understanding what *posse comitatus* might mean for the enforcement of civil rights in the South, but, since he clings to an outmoded chronological definition of Reconstruction, he fails to take the final step.[27]

Only the 1941 study by the Brookings Institute fully discerns the expansive possibilities of federal intervention after the *posse comitatus* restrictions entered federal law in 1878. The evident wonderment with which its author, Bennett Rich, reached this conclusion is in itself compelling evidence of a path not taken. After moving through a synopsis of the federal statutes relating to insurrection, Rich noted the existence of a federal law "that has received singularly little attention." At this point, he then inserted the complete text of Revised Statute 5299, the same one left out of the Leavenworth analysis. While noting that "writers dealing with the subject have done little more than recognize the existence of this statute" (pointing to 1940 research on presidential power by a noted constitutional law scholar), Rich correctly perceived its potential reach: "Into the hands of the president is placed the power of determining whether, by insurrection, domestic violence, unlawful combinations, or conspiracies, any portion or class of the people of a state is being deprived of the 'rights privileges, or immunities, or protection, named in the Constitution and secured by the laws'. . . . Under such circumstances the president is authorized to use the military forces of the United States to correct the evil." Although he observed that "no president has based his action in handling a disturbance exclusively on R.S.

5299," and regarded it as unlikely that any large-scale disorder that might activate the act would not also allow for federal intervention under other statutes, Rich ended his discussion of the issue by concluding that "R.S. 5299 is an additional weapon in the president's hands to guard against the dangers of widespread and unchecked oppression of minority groups."[28]

This 1941 study plays the role of Cassandra in analyses of *posse comitatus*, as it alone among those few studies grappling with the "expressly authorized" exemptions to *posse comitatus* carved out by Congress has gleaned a vital point. Through Section 3 of the 3rd Enforcement Act (1871), Congress not only authorized but insisted that the president use military force "for the suppression of such insurrection, domestic violence, or combinations" that served to "deprive any portion or class of the people ... of any of the rights, privileges, and immunities, or protection, named in the Constitution and secured by this act" whenever state and local officials "shall either be unable to protect, or shall, from any cause, fail in or refuse protection of the people in such rights." Be it through acts of commission or omission (the latter being the "state neglect" theory of civil rights enforcement, articulated by the Supreme Court in the 1870s and 1880s, that Pamela Brandwein has cogently resurrected from historical oblivion), the failure of nonfederal officials to secure mandated rights for all would "be deemed a denial by such State of the equal protection of the laws to which they are entitled."[29] This section of the 3rd Enforcement Act survived every legal assault upon Reconstruction launched in the 1870s and beyond, ended up in the Revised Statutes of 1874 and 1878 as Revised Statute 5299, and became part of the modern United States Code in the 1920s, where it lay dormant until the Department of Justice used it as the primary legal justification for federal intervention throughout the civil rights movement, starting with the 1957 crisis over school segregation involving the Little Rock Nine. In other words, nothing changed in federal law between 1871 and 1957 to permit federal intervention on behalf of African American civil rights; what changed was the political calculus surrounding that intervention.

The best place to begin to demonstrate this point is the statutory language of the Army Appropriations Act as it relates to *posse comitatus*. Many scholars who write on the subject have not actually examined the language of Section 15 or tracked down the contemporary discussion concerning it; instead, they have unwittingly repeated a slanted Democratic Party interpretation of Section 15 that was codified in the historical profession by the Dunning School of the early twentieth century. (A similar development applies to our understanding of the key Supreme Court decisions on civil rights from *Slaughter House* on, as Pamela Brandwein has meticulously shown.)[30] Adopting the Democratic Party perspective, which insisted that all future use of the military as domestic law enforcement was illegal, has led scholars to miss the vital center of Section 15, which is captured in the modifying clause "except in such cases and under such circumstances as such employment of said force may be expressly authorized by the Constitution or by act of Congress." This clause immediately carved out a series of statutory exceptions to the seemingly blanket prohibition on the use of the army as domestic law enforcement. Indeed, the existence of this clause is the reason Republicans in the Senate finally acceded to revising the *posse comitatus* policy—it was the cost they extracted for agreeing to the restrictions in the first place. While not depicted as such in the literature (apart from a brief reference in Ari Hoogenboom's history of the Hayes administration), the denouement of the *posse comitatus* debate could even be read as a Republican victory, since the Republicans prevented Democrats from "crippl[ing] the Reconstruction amendments," given the number and reach of these existing exemptions now codified in federal law.[31]

Precisely which exemptions existed at the time the 1878 Army Appropriations Act entered into federal law? The general-in-chief of the army, William Tecumseh Sherman, helpfully delineated these in General Orders No. 49 and 71, issued after the new *posse comitatus* policy had become federal law.[32] Eighteen statutes from the newly *Revised Statutes of the United States* represented preexisting exemptions from Congress's action on *posse comitatus*. Some of these statutes referred to extremely specific circumstances: discoverers of "guano islands," for example, were assured that the president could "employ the land and naval forces of the United States" to protect their domains, a law that remains in effect today.[33] Other exemptions related to broader topics—Indian Country, Neutrality Act provisions, and extradition procedures, for example. Not surprisingly, given the legal edifice constructed by the Republican Party during Congressional Reconstruction, a few sections dealt with civil rights. But the aforementioned Section 3 of the 3rd Enforcement Act was not listed among them. Instead, as befitting its placement in the *Revised Statutes*, Section 3 was listed as a statutory exception stemming from *Title LXIX: Insurrection.*[34]

The migration of an important component of a bill enacted to "secure the rights guaranteed by section 1" of the Fourteenth Amendment into a portion of the *Revised Statutes* otherwise devoted to a series of Insurrection Acts (passed in the early republic and updated during the early days of the Civil War) is explicable, but not necessarily rational.[35] When Congress authorized the creation of the *Revised Statutes* in the early 1870s, it seems clear that it did not intend that those persons undertaking the work would do anything more than reorganize the vast body of federal law. Yet, in practice, the commissioners in charge of the project removed sections of laws, compressed them, or altered their wording, actions that had an impact on at least one Supreme Court decision on civil rights.[36] This was, perhaps, an inevitable by-product of a rushed process. It may be that those creating the *Revised Statutes* placed Section 3 of the 3rd Enforcement Act among the Insurrection statutes, because the section referenced "insurrection" in its first sentence ("Whenever insurrection, domestic violence, unlawful combinations, or conspiracies in any State so obstructs or hinders the execution of the laws thereof, and of the United States . . ."); however, the language of the bill listed "insurrection" as only one of many possible forms of violence. Whatever the reasoning behind the move, placing Section 3 into the Insurrection statutes (where it became Revised Statute 5299) may have shielded it from the Democratic Party's counterattack on Reconstruction.

Whether or not this proved to be the case, Section 5299 not only survived the nineteenth century unscathed but came to serve as perhaps the most far-reaching exception to the ban on the use of the army as a *posse comitatus.* The significance of this development has not been fully appreciated. In short, regardless of the congressional restrictions placed on the army's powers to function as a *posse comitatus* in 1878, the United States Army, at the direction of the president, retained the statutory authority to intervene in civil society to prevent civil rights violations. This power did not stem from a tortured construction of vague statutory language, nor was it esoteric to contemporary observers, as events in the fall of 1878 demonstrated.

In late October 1878, the *New York Times* published a remarkable editorial that boldly spelled out the contours of the federal prerogative after the canonical end of Reconstruction. What prompted the article was "the bold and systematic manner in which a certain class of citizens of the United States are deprived of their vested rights in some of the Southern states"—in other words, the regular rounds of violence, coercion, and intimidation that preceded an important national election.[37] Rather than reacting "with scarcely a shrug, [abandoning] the freedpeople of the South to their fate," as has been asserted about the North's reaction to the Compromise of 1877, the *Times* editorial insisted that Reconstruction was far from over.[38] Significantly, it recognized that any discussion of federal countermeasures had to grapple with *posse comitatus:*

> There can be no doubt that the *posse comitatus* clause of the Army Appropriations act, passed at the last session of Congress, has emboldened the Southern Democrats in their present unlawful crusade against the Republicans of that section, the prevailing idea being that the clause effectively prohibits the National Government from using its authority to interfere with them, unless upon the call of the Governors of the respective States for federal assistance. . . . The purpose of the Democrats was to prevent the Army from being used to protect citizens from just such persecution as is now prevailing in South Carolina. The intimidation of unoffending colored men in the South is the effect of that clause, and it was intended to have that effect.

However, the *Times* editorial maintained, the Democrats, had failed to accomplish their intended ends, because any construction of *posse comitatus* holding that the military could no longer be used in such a fashion misread federal law. "A careful examination of the Revised Statutes," the editorial concluded, "justifies the opinion that the *posse comitatus* clause does not prevent the President from using the military forces of the United States to prevent the outrages as are now being perpetuated in South Carolina through the connivance, if not with the sanction, of the State authorities." This is because, as written, Section 15 of the Army Appropriations Act "expressly provided that the Army may be employed" when authorized to do so by the Constitution or prior act of Congress. Chief among these existing laws was Revised Statute 5298, an insurrection statute whose origins lay in the early republic. "But, if it be contended that the section above . . . refers only to active insurrection against the United States," the *Times* continued, then supporters of federal intervention could find relief elsewhere: "it will not be denied that the act of April 20, 1871 (see Revised Statutes, section 5,299) gives the President ample authority to act in such cases as are now presented by daily occurrences in South Carolina." At this point, the *Times* then quoted the whole of Revised Statute 5299, italicizing the phrase "*it shall be lawful for the President of the United States and it shall be his duty*" to use military force to suppress civil rights violations. Far from throwing up one's hands in despair at the government's inability to change this sad state of the affairs in the South, the *Times* determined that an aggressive response to Southern outrages was not only warranted, but completely lawful.[39]

Editorials like these must have sent shivers down the spines of Democrats eager to consolidate their emerging, but vigorously contested, control of the South. As the *Times* put it, "Here is a law which fits the case of South Carolina as nicely as though specially made for it. Indeed if Congress was now in session and disposed to redress the wrongs imposed on unoffending citizens by the Democracy of that State, no more positive language could be employed and no more effective statute framed." Even if chastened Republican leaders avoided using intervention wantonly, as Charles Calhoun has argued, "they still embraced the threat of intervention by a Republican administration as a kind of latent power that could force southerners into moderately good behavior."[40] While this intervention might occur anywhere in the United States, everyone knew that the violent opposition of white Southerners to the policies of Congressional Reconstruction had prompted Congress to act in the first place, and both parties realized that the prospect of federal intervention into the affairs of the South remained a live possibility. Republicans, in fact, to use the words of James Hogue, "threatened the South with the specter of another military intervention" through the early 1890s. This represented an existential threat to the Democratic Party, which relied upon white Southerners to remain competitive in national elections.[41]

Aware that Republicans still contemplated federal intervention to secure the fruits of Reconstruction, Democrats responded with force in the South and with parliamentary maneuvers in Washington. While practically all of the scholarly literature on *posse comitatus* views the 1878 act as a watershed event, Democrats living in the shadow of that act regularly tried to undo their accomplishment by revising the *posse comitatus* language they had approved in the hope of ending the use of the military as a *posse comitatus* once and for all. Notably, their quest to eliminate the prospect of military intervention on behalf of civil rights played out *after* the restrictions on *posse comitatus* had, according to most of today's scholars, permanently ended the military's role in enforcing domestic law. For example, a year after the *posse comitatus* restrictions became law, Democrats launched a renewed effort to limit the ability of the military to preserve peace at the polls during federal elections; in this quest, they used both riders and an actual bill, only to see both vetoed.[42] Concern over potential federal intervention also explains the party's dogged attempts to repeal the Enforcement Acts, a battle in which they failed to make headway until 1894, nearly a generation after the Compromise of 1877. If the Supreme Court decisions of the 1870s and 1880s had fatally eviscerated federal attempts to protect the civil rights of African Americans, and if the *posse comitatus* restrictions had eliminated the ability of the military to intervene in Southern affairs, why did the Democratic Party spend so much time and energy trying to repeal acts of Congress theoretically invalidated by the Supreme Court and to change the party's own *posse comitatus* language?[43]

The basic implication of all this is, hopefully, quite clear: the same legal framework that permitted federal intervention during the civil rights movement of the mid-twentieth century existed during and after Reconstruction. Instead of being proscribed, federal intervention in the South remained possible. In the end, it suffered a fate akin to that experienced by agents of the Freedmen's Bureau, whose labors faltered, as Robert Kaczorowski concludes, not because of "the insufficiency of national civil rights law," but because of "an insufficiency of political power and failure of will" by national leaders.[44] The cadre of eminent law school professors who chided the Kennedy administration for claiming that it lacked the authority to intervene during Freedom Summer could have been speaking about any presidential administration from Grant on when they pointedly concluded, "it is not lack of Presidential power to act but the absence of a conviction that action is now called for that explains nonaction." Or, as the *New York Times* pointedly wondered in 1878: "The President is not only clothed with ample authority to protect the people of South Carolina in all their lawful rights, but it is made his duty, under his oath of office, to adopt such measures as he may deem necessary to do so. Will he do it?"[45]

Of course, even had President Hayes—or any of his successors—decided on this course of action, one cannot automatically assume that the army would have been zealous or effective in its duties. As several scholars have pointed out, the post–Civil War United States Army suffered from a host of basic deficiencies, ranging from small budgets and lackadaisical training regimens to a confused command structure and a paucity of strategic thinking.[46] Moreover, as Joseph Dawson shows in his study of the army's experience in reconstructing Louisiana, the political leanings of commanders opposed to Reconstruction could and did hamstring federal attempts to protect civil and political rights in the South, as when Henry Halleck, commander of the Department of the South, inserted an extra layer of bureaucracy into the *posse comitatus* process, thereby weakening it.[47] Despite these factors, however, reasons also exist to reach a more sanguine conclusion.

If one approaches the question of military intervention into civil society by thinking about the broader history of war and society in the nineteenth century, one will discover reasons for optimism. While the army frequently intervened in civil society after the Civil War thanks to its standing as the sole federal agency with a national reach, such actions unfolded without serious opposition, even if they were not exactly popular. While low-grade harassment, including lawsuits filed against commanders, did take place, not even the strenuous challenges of pacifying the South during Reconstruction, maintaining the boundaries of Indian reservations from incursions by white squatters in the trans-Mississippi West, and quelling violence during the general strike of 1877 led to violence between civilians and federal troops.[48] As Coakley's comprehensive account of the army's activities during Reconstruction concludes, "A striking feature of this whole unusual experience ... was the success achieved by small contingents of troops in controlling violence where far larger numbers of rioters were involved."[49] More than one historian has argued that the absence of violence stemmed from not only the superior discipline of regulars but also the moral authority the army possessed among Northern civilians—many veterans themselves—as the formal representative of the national government.[50] In the South, the trend remained the same, but the calculus differed. Despite the repugnance with which they viewed Reconstruction, the diverse forces opposing it generally avoided conflict with federal soldiers because they feared inciting a more aggressive federal response. For example, even as Reconstruction broke down on the northern fringes of Louisiana in 1874, a region where local authorities had gone to the extreme of seizing a young lieutenant and trying him on trumped-up charges in a state court, a colonel of infantry sent to investigate the situation there emphasized that local whites had "*not the slightest disposition to oppose the General Government.*"[51] As Southerners knew all too well, that had been tried and it had failed, killing in the process approximately 13 percent of white men of military age born in slave states.[52]

Intervention of the sort envisioned by both the 3rd Enforcement Act and the *posse comitatus* policy would not have been easy. There is good reason to suspect that, had such intervention been applied, its harsher aspects would have been softened by the strength of local elites, the difficulty of the mission, budgetary and manpower shortfalls, the lack of coordination across the federal bureaucracy, and occasional incompetence on the part of local commanders.[53] Still, given the virulence with which the Democratic Party sought to weaken the federal army during this period—seeking to reduce its numbers, resisting compromise in Congress (with the end result that the army was not paid during several years in the 1870s), and trying to rein in its ability to intervene in civil society—it stands to reason that the army hit a vital Southern nerve.

With the backing of both arms and federal law, it promised a modicum of protection for African Americans, and the threat of persecution for those opposed to Reconstruction. In the final analysis, as James Sefton states, even though "frequent changes in federal policy" during Reconstruction kept the "legal power and functions" of the army in constant flux, "one of the most noteworthy aspects of the Army's activity in the South was its ability as an institution to adjust to these changes in policy." With an institutional history filled with examples of its work in the service of controversial domestic initiatives, the U.S. Army might well have been the outside center of power required to fulfill the basic mission of Congressional Reconstruction by helping to bring to maturity an uneasy new world in the states of the former Confederacy.[54]

While various levels of government lurched toward a disorganized and chaotic response in the face of the epic devastation wrought by Hurricane Katrina in September 2005, many Americans wondered why the nation's military had not rapidly deployed to the disaster zone. In response, administration officials hastened to assure reporters that, much as they wanted to, they could not have taken charge of the relief response without the approval of Louisiana's governor. Since that approval was not forthcoming, they argued, they lacked the requisite authority to do so.[55] William C. Banks, an authority on *posse comitatus* law, stated that these assertions were wrong, because any limitations upon the military's ability to intervene in American society "are more cultural than legal." According to the *New York Times*, Banks "said Mr. Bush's authority extended to using the troops to stop looting—a law enforcement function—under provisions that enable him to put down any act of insurrection."[56]

Section 3 of the 3rd Enforcement Act, also known as Revised Statute 5299, otherwise known as Title 10, U.S. Code §333, had made an appearance again. It had, after all, never gone away, even if it had lain "long-dormant and little-discussed" for much of its history. White Southerners opposed to equal citizenship and equal rights for black Americans—the original targets of the statutory language—only discovered how serious the radical Republicans were in the 1950s and 1960s, when the Department of Justice in both the Eisenhower and Kennedy administrations invoked §333 as the primary legal justification for the federal response to civil rights violations and the forces of white supremacy in the South.[57] Fittingly, the democratic promise of Reconstruction, so long deferred, would play out on new Southern battlefields—Little Rock, Montgomery, Oxford, Tuscaloosa, Birmingham, the Mississippi Delta, and Selma—using a very old rubric.

1. The articles found in a special issue of the *Cleveland State Law Review* constitute an important exception. See "Kent State 1970—Legal Background and Implications," *Cleveland State Law Review* 22, no. 1 (Winter 1973).

2. "Kent State: Martyrdom That Shook the Country," *Time*, May 18, 1970, 12–14; Andrew Huebner, *The Warrior Image: Soldiers in American Culture from the Second World War to the Vietnam Era* (Chapel Hill: Univ. of North Carolina Press, 2008), 215, 217, 239, 253. See also Tom Englehardt, *The End of Victory Culture: Cold War America and the Disillusioning of a Generation*, rev. and expanded ed. (Amherst: Univ. of Massachusetts Press, 2007).

3. Clayton D. Laurie, "Filling the Breach: Military Aid to the Civil Power in the Trans-Mississippi West," *Western Historical Quarterly* 25, no. 2 (1994): 156.

4. Michael L. Tate, *The Frontier Army in the Settlement of the West* (Norman: Univ. of Oklahoma Press, 1999), 81

5. John Phillip Reid, *In Defiance of the Law: The Standing-Army Controversy, The Two Constitutions, and the Coming of the American Revolution* (Chapel Hill: Univ. of North Carolina Press, 1981), 88–91, Lord Bathurst qtd. on 94

6. Ibid., 6–7.

7. Caleb Cushing, qtd. in U.S. Library of Congress, Congressional Research Service (hereafter, CRS), *The Posse Comitatus Act and Related Matters: The Use of the Military to Execute Civilian Law*, by Charles Doyle and Jennifer Elsea, R42659 (2012), 17.

8. Tate, *Frontier Army*, 81–83. The best overviews of the history of *posse comitatus* in the American context can be found in Robert W. Coakley, *The Role of Federal Military Forces in Domestic Disorders, 1789–1878* (Washington, D.C.: U.S. Army Center of Military History, 1989); and U.S. Library of Congress, CRS, *The Posse Comitatus Act and Related Matters: Use of the Military*.

9. Tate, *Frontier Army*, 81–82; Laurie, "Filling the Breach," 149; *Posse Comitatus Act and Related Matters*, 15–16; and Tate, *Frontier Army*, 81–82, 95–110. For an older, but still valuable, discussion of the difficult time the U.S. Army had enforcing the law in the face of unruly settlers, see Francis Paul Prucha, *Broadax and Bayonet: The Role of the United States Army in the Development of the Old Northwest*, 2nd ed. (Lincoln: Univ. of Nebraska Press, 1995). A more modern exposition of this theme can be found throughout Samuel Watson, *Peacekeepers and Conquerors: The Army Officer Corps on the Frontier, 1821–1846* (Lawrence: Univ. Press of Kansas, 2013).

10. Leonard White, *The Republican Era: A Study in Administrative History, 1869–1901* (New York: MacMillan, 1958), 35–39. Oddly enough, even though White recognized the Democratic thrust to curtail federal protection of civil and political rights in the South, he completely missed the debate over the army's *posse comitatus* powers.

11. *An Act Making Appropriations for the Support of the Army for the Fiscal Year Ending June Thirtieth, Eighteen Hundred and Seventy-Nine, and for Other Purposes, U.S. Statutes at Large* 20 (1878): 152.

12. "Posse Comitatus," *The West Wing*, first broadcast May 22, 2002, by NBC, directed by Alex Graves and written by Aaron Sorkin.

13. See, for example, David E. Sanger, "Bush Wants to Consider Broadening of Military's Powers During Natural Disasters," *New York Times*, Sept. 27, 2005, accessed Sept. 14, 2014, <http://www.nytimes.com/2005/09/27/national/nationalspecial/27military.html?_r=0>.

14. Mark Bradley, *Bluecoats and Tar Heels: Soldiers and Civilians in Reconstruction North Carolina* (Lexington: Univ. Press of Kentucky, 2009), 257; James Hogue, *Uncivil War: Five New Orleans Street Battles and the Rise and Fall of Radical Reconstruction* (Baton Rouge: Louisiana State Univ. Press, 2006), 181–83. As Hogue cogently puts it, Democrats "operated under the simple yet plausible assumption that if there was not much of a federal army, there could not be much intervention in southern affairs" (181).

15. Eric Foner, *Reconstruction: America's Unfinished Revolution, 1863–1877* (New York: Harper and Row, 1988), 686; Michael Fitzgerald, *Splendid Failure: Postwar Reconstruction and the American South* (Chicago, Ill.: Ivan R. Dee, 2006).

16. William A. Blair, "The Use of Military Force to Defend the Gains of Reconstruction," *Civil War History* 51, no. 4 (2005): 388–402.

17. Michael Vorenberg, "Reconstruction as a Constitutional Crisis," in *Reconstructions: New Perspectives on the Postbellum United States,* ed. Thomas J. Brown (New York: Oxford Univ. Press, 2006).

18. Joseph Dawson, *Army Generals and Reconstruction: Louisiana, 1862–1877* (Baton Rouge: Louisiana State Univ. Press, 1982), 1. Two essays, Blair's "The Use of Military Force," and Andrew Lang's "Republicanism, Race, and Reconstruction: The Ethos of Military Occupation in Civil War America," *Journal of the Civil War Era* 4, no. 4 (Dec. 2014): 449–89, are rare exceptions, although the authors of both are pessimistic about a long-term military occupation of the South. Greg Downs's important recent study, *After Appomattox: Military Occupation and the Ends of War* (Cambridge, Mass.: Harvard Univ. Press, 2015), places military occupation at the center of Reconstruction. While *After Appomattox* does not reach its full potential because of its emphasis on the already well-studied highest command levels of the U.S. Army and because it ends its discussion of military affairs in 1871, it hopefully will inspire more work on the military side of Reconstruction.

19. Charles W. Calhoun, *Conceiving a New Republic: The Republican Party and the Southern Question, 1869–1900* (Lawrence: Univ. Press of Kansas, 2006), esp. 161–200. A condensed version of Calhoun's thinking on sectional politics can be found in Charles W. Calhoun, *From Bloody Shirt to Full Dinner Pail: The Transformation of Politics and Governance in the Gilded Age* (New York: Hill and Wang, 2010).

20. Ari Hoogenboom, *Rutherford B. Hayes: Warrior and President* (Lawrence: Univ. Press of Kansas, 1995), 352, 376, 393–98.

21. Scholars of American political development have (surprisingly) failed to pay much attention to the army, but Stephen Skowronek provides a good summation of the political process by which *posse comitatus* restrictions emerged, along with a discussion of later attempts to constrain the army's domestic operations and a consideration of the implication of these restrictions for urban disorder. See Stephen Skowronek, *Building a New American State: The Expansion of National Administrative Capacities, 1877–1920* (New York: Cambridge Univ. Press, 1982), 102–3, 319n.51.

22. James Sefton, *The United States Army and Reconstruction, 1865–1877* (Baton Rouge: Louisiana State Univ. Press, 1967); Jerry Cooper, *The Army and Civil Disorder: Federal Intervention in Labor Disputes, 1877–1900* (Westport, Conn.: Greenwood Press, 1980), 83–84, 241–42.

23. Robert Wooster, *The American Military Frontiers: The United States Army in the West, 1783–1900* (Albuquerque: Univ. of New Mexico Press, 2009), 243, 246. Two of Wooster's other studies of the frontier army fail to mention *posse comitatus* at all. See Robert Wooster,

The Military and United States Indian Policy, 1865–1903 (New Haven, Conn.: Yale Univ. Press, 1988) and *Nelson A. Miles and the Twilight of the Frontier Army* (Lincoln: Univ. of Nebraska Press, 1993).

24. Tate, *Frontier Army in the Settlement of the West,* 94, 109–10.

25. William Birkhimer, *Military Government and Martial Law,* 3rd ed., rev. (Kansas City, Mo.: Franklin Hudson Publishing Co., 1914), 490, 502–7; Cassius M. Dowell, *Military Aid to the Civil Power* (Ft. Leavenworth, Kans.: General Service Schools Press, 1925), 203–10.

26. Here it should be noted that the CRS report on *posse comitatus* cited in note 8 above explicitly notes the Enforcement Act exception, but as a reference work it is not considered here. See U.S. Library of Congress, CRS, *The Posse Comitatus Act and Related Matters: Use of the Military,* 15.

27. Coakley, *The Role of Federal Military Forces,* 344–45. The prevalent notion that federal forces immediately withdrew from the South after the Compromise of 1877 is erroneous; see Clarence C. Clenden, "President Hayes' 'Withdrawal' of the Troops: An Enduring Myth," *The South Carolina Historical Magazine* 70, no. 4 (1969): 240–50.

28. Bennett Milton Rich, *The Presidents and Civil Disorder* (Washington D.C.: Brookings Institution, 1941), 198–201.

29. *An Act to Enforce the Provisions of the Fourteenth Amendment to the Constitution of the United States, and or Other Purposes, U.S. Statutes at Large* 17 (1871): 14; Pamela Brandwein, *Rethinking the Judicial Settlement of Reconstruction* (New York: Cambridge Univ. Press, 2011), 11–14.

30. Brandwein, *Rethinking the Judicial Settlement,* 222–23, 227–39. For a representative example of the Dunning School's dismissive tone toward the federal effort to protect civil rights in the South and its confident assertion that the Enforcement Acts "are practically dead letters" with only "seven slightly important sections" surviving the counterattack on Reconstruction, see William Watson Davis, "The Federal Enforcement Acts," in *Studies in Southern History and Politics, Inscribed to William Archibald Dunning* (New York: Columbia Univ. Press, 1914), 205–28.

31. Hoogenboom, *Warrior and President,* 352.

32. Sherman's second order added new exemptions concerning quarantines and extradition while clarifying when officers might intervene without presidential authorization. See Adjutant General's Office, General Orders No. 49 and 71, *Index of General Orders, 1878* (Washington, D.C.: GPO, 1879). It should be noted that Sherman listed article 4, section 4 of the Constitution as an important exemption to the new *posse comitatus* policy; this section guarantees "to every State in this Union a republican form of government" and proclaims that the federal government "shall protect each of them against invasion; and on application of the legislature, or of the executive (when the legislature cannot be convened), against domestic violence." Many, though not all, Republicans identified this part of the Constitution as a founding principle that not only justified the expansion of suffrage and civil rights to African Americans but also validated federal intervention to secure this expansion. See Calhoun, *Conceiving a New Republic,* 15–16, 21, 28.

33. *Revised Statutes of the United States,* 2nd ed. (Washington, D.C.: GPO, 1878), 1081. For those seeking the guano islands provision in today's *United States Code, see Employment of Land and Naval Forces in Protection of Rights,* §1418 in Chapter 8, Guano Islands, Title 48, *United States Code.*

34. Adjutant General's Office, General Orders No. 49 and 71, *Index of General Orders, 1878,* 1029.

35. "Federal Intervention in the States," 419–21. For a complete list of the statutes in the Insurrection title, see *Revised Statutes*, 1029–34.

36. "Federal Intervention in the States," 456n.152; Brandwein, *Rethinking the Judicial Settlement*, 123–26.

37. "The President's Power and Duty," *New York Times*, Oct. 28, 1878.

38. William Wiececk, *The Lost World of Classical Legal Thought: Law and Ideology in America, 1886–1937* (New York: Oxford Univ. Press, 1998), 77; Brandwein, *Rethinking the Judicial Settlement*, 1–7.

39. "The President's Power and Duty."

40. "The President's Power and Duty"; Calhoun, *Conceiving a New Republic*, 91. Federal intervention on behalf of African American voting rights in the South remained a reality in the late 1870s and early 1880s, as the Hayes, Garfield, and Arthur administrations deployed hundreds of federal marshals to the South during elections and dramatically expanded Enforcement Act prosecutions. See Brandwein, *Rethinking the Judicial Settlement*, 88, 129, 142–44. Federal action on behalf of civil rights occasionally occurred outside the South as well: in 1885 and 1886, the Cleveland administration used the legal framework described above to deploy the U.S. Army to the Pacific Northwest on behalf of Chinese victims of white mobs. It also brought federal civil rights charges against mob leaders, although it failed to secure convictions. See Kevin Adams, "'The failure was signal': The U.S. Army and the Anti-Chinese Riots in Seattle" (presentation, Western Historical Association annual meeting, Tucson, Ariz., Oct. 2013).

41. Hogue, *Uncivil War*, 181.

42. Calhoun, *Conceiving a New Republic*, 161–68; Hoogenboom, *Warrior and President*, 392–99.

43. Brandwein asks a related question from the perspective of the Republican Party: if the Supreme Court decisions of the 1870s and 1880s served as the coup de grace for Reconstruction, why did Republican agitation for African American rights continue until the early 1890s? See Brandwein, *Rethinking the Judicial Settlement*, 10. For a "state of the field" assessment of the fluid endpoint for Reconstruction, see "Historians' Forum: Reconstruction," *Civil War History* 61, no. 3 (Sept. 2015): 281–301.

44. Robert Kaczorowski, *The Politics of Judicial Interpretation: The Federal Courts, Department of Justice, and Civil Rights, 1866–1876*, 2nd ed. (New York: Fordham Univ. Press, 2005), 21.

45. Qtd. in John H. Fenton, "29 Jurists, Disputing Kennedy, Say U.S. Can Act in Mississippi," *New York Times*, July 1, 1964, accessed Dec. 2, 2014, <http://www.nytimes.com/1964/07/01/29-jurists-disputing-kennedy-say-us-can-act-in-mississippi.html>; "The President's Power and Duty."

46. Kevin Adams, *Class and Race in the Frontier Army: Military Life in the West, 1870–1890* (Norman: Univ. of Oklahoma Press, 2009), 64–72. Good introductions to the strengths and faults of the post–Civil War army can be found in Wooster, *The Military and United States Indian Policy*, and his *Nelson A. Miles and the Twilight of the Frontier Army;* Paul Hutton, *Phil Sheridan and His Army* (Lincoln: Univ. of Nebraska Press, 1985); Jack D. Foner, *The United States Soldier Between Two Wars: Army Life and Reforms, 1865–1898* (New York: Humanities Press, 1970); Robert Utley, *Frontier Regulars: The United States Army and the Indian, 1866–1891* (New York: MacMillan, 1974); Edward Coffman, *The Old Army: A Portrait of the American Army in Peacetime, 1784–1898* (New York: Oxford Univ. Press, 1986); and Tate, *The Frontier Army in the Settlement of the West*.

47. Dawson, *Army Generals and Reconstruction*, 1; Richard Zuczek, *State of Rebellion: Reconstruction in South Carolina* (Columbia: Univ. of South Carolina Press, 1996), 81. Dawson demonstrates that there was no monolithic army viewpoint on Reconstruction, as generals could enforce the dictates of Reconstruction policy, obstruct them openly, or vacillate toward them depending on their personal inclinations and capabilities.

48. Kevin Adams and Khal Schneider, "'Washington is a Long Way Off': The Round Valley War and the Limits of Federal Power on a California Indian Reservation," *Pacific Historical Review* 80, no. 4 (Nov. 2011): 557–96.

49. Coakley, *The Role of Federal Military Forces*, 341, 348.

50. Cooper, *Army and Civil Disorder*, 60–61.

51. Dawson, *Army Generals and Reconstruction*, 190–95 (italics in original).

52. J. David Hacker, "A Census-Based Count of the Civil War Dead," *Civil War History* 57, no. 4 (Dec. 2011): 342.

53. For illustrations of how the army's capacity to enforce federal dictates could be eroded by local realities, see Adams and Schneider, "'Washington is a Long Way Off'"; Jeffrey Ostler, *The Plains Sioux and U.S. Colonialism* (New York: Cambridge Univ. Press, 2004), esp. 40–84; and Elliott West, *The Last Indian War: The Nez Perce Story* (New York: Oxford Univ. Press, 2009).

54. Sefton, *The United States Army and Reconstruction*, 253.

55. Eric Lipton, Eric Schmitt, and Thom Shanker, "Political Issues Snarled Plans for Troop Aid," *New York Times*, Sept. 9, 2005, accessed Sept. 17, 2014, <http://www.nytimes.com/2005/09/09/national/nationalspecial/09military.html?pagewanted=1>; Sanger, "Broadening of Military's Powers."

56. William C. Banks, qtd. in David E. Sanger, "Bush Wants to Consider Broadening of Military's Powers During Natural Disasters," *New York Times*, Sept. 27, 2005, accessed Sept. 17, 2014, < http://www.nytimes.com/2005/09/27/us/nationalspecial/bush-wants-to-consider-broadening-of-militarys-powers-during-natural-disasters.html>.

57. "Federal Intervention in the States for the Suppression of Domestic Violence: Constitutionality, Statutory Power, and Policy," *Duke Law Journal* 15, no. 2 (1966): 415–19, quote on 415. The Kennedy administration, in particular, invoked §333 only after considerable foot-dragging and denial of the federal government's ability to act. See the article cited above, as well as Fenton, "29 Jurists."

Democracy and Race in the Late Reconstruction South

The White Leagues of Louisiana

Mitchell Snay

The struggle over democracy remains a central theme in nineteenth-century American history. In the Early Republic, the ideological legacies of the Revolution, the rise of a market economy, and the expansion of white male suffrage collectively democratized American life. "The people reign in the political world," Alexis de Tocqueville noted during his visit to the United States during the 1830s, "as the Deity does in the Universe." The Civil War and Reconstruction extended beyond racial boundaries by freeing the slaves and adding the Thirteenth, Fourteenth, and Fifteenth Amendments to the Constitution. Voting participation expanded to new heights during the Gilded Age that followed. Toward the end of the century, the populist movement again challenged Americans to live up to their democratic ideals, a struggle that continued during the Progressive Era.[1]

Yet various forces curbed the trend toward democracy during the nineteenth century. Vestiges of aristocratic political and social orders endured in places like New York's Hudson River Valley and the lowcountry of South Carolina. Paradoxically, the economic transformations that opened up new opportunities also generated inequalities in wealth distribution. The rapid growth of industrial capitalism fostered a stratified social order that threatened the democratic ideal. Additionally, some Americans questioned the wisdom of popular sovereignty. In 1869, the New York *Journal of Commerce* stated openly that the "tendency among thoughtful men who desire honesty, economy, and a good deal of intelligence in legislation is towards a restriction of the right of suffrage considerably inside its present limits."[2]

The conflict between democratic and antidemocratic impulses was especially poignant in the American South. During the Revolutionary Era, as historian Edmund S. Morgan showed brilliantly in the mid-1970s, the rise of American freedom in the South was accompanied by a growing commitment to chattel slavery. By the nineteenth century, however, the South was defined by a fierce egalitarianism among the Southern yeomanry and a tradition of *herrenvolk* democracy, in which whites constructed an ideology of equality within their own race that served to mask inequalities and class conflicts among them. When lower-class whites challenged the hegemony of wealthy planters and merchants, white elites raised the bugbear of racial equality and amalgamation. At the same time, they took efforts to restrict voting, not only by blacks but by some whites as well.[3]

Perhaps at no other time was the conflict over democracy as intense as during the era of Reconstruction (1865–77). The place of the African American in American life was the central question in politics after the Civil War. To what extent was American democracy to be expanded to include blacks? Reconstruction also raised thorny problems about suffrage. How far would the federal government go to protect American citizens seeking to exercise their rights of suffrage? Should former Confederates be disfranchised?

The problems of democracy in the late Reconstruction South can be profitably explored by looking at the White League of Louisiana. At first glance, it would seem odd to look for democracy in a violent white supremacist group. Yet sources on the league reveal class tensions among whites. Rather than simply unifying Southern whites along lines of race, these sources suggest that moments of heightened racial consciousness might have opened a door for farmers and laborers to challenge the supremacy of men of property.[4]

I.

The White League of Louisiana played an infamous role in the drama of Reconstruction. Originating in 1874 in opposition to Gov. William P. Kellogg, a Radical Republican, it was instrumental in the overthrow of the Republican government in Louisiana. The first White League meeting took place in Opelousas on April 27. Another chapter was formed in New Orleans months later. There is also evidence of White League activity in the neighboring states of Mississippi, Arkansas, and Texas. The Louisiana White League engaged in a campaign of intimidation and violence against the Republicans, suspending local Republican governance, harassing African American workers, and targeting Republican officeholders for assassination. Its members were responsible for two of the most violent episodes associated with the end of Reconstruction in Louisiana—the Coushatta Massacre of August 27, 1874, and the Battle of Liberty Place in New Orleans on September 14 of that year. The goal of the White League, as summed up in a letter by E. T. Lewis, one of its leaders, was "to place the control of the State in the hands of white men, and to combine upon this as the leading object to be accomplished." The White League was successful in meeting this goal. In April 1877, federal troops who had been supporting Gov. Kellogg's administration were withdrawn under orders from President Rutherford B. Hayes. Reconstruction in America had come to an ignoble end.[5]

In several key ways, the White League continued the pattern of violent racial repression established earlier during Reconstruction. Most obvious were its similarities to the Ku Klux Klan. Like the Klan, the White League resisted black aspirations to communal autonomy, economic independence, and political equality. The league's propensity to violence has been well documented. In August 1874, a mob of league members caught and shot African American political leader Eli Allen, broke his arms and legs, and tortured him over a fire until he died. Perhaps the most notorious episode of league violence concerns native New Englander Marshall H. Twitchell, who in the 1870s served as a courageous Republican leader in Louisiana's Red River Parish. Already by 1874, Twitchell had suffered the deaths of his wife and young son Daniel. At the end of July 1874, White League activity in the Red River area forced Twitchell to travel to New Orleans, where he appealed in vain for federal troops to support local Republican officials. On August 31, 1874, while he was recovering from his fruitless efforts at a friend's house in Mississippi, he learned that his brother Homer and two brothers-in-law had been among many whites and blacks murdered by White Leaguers in an attack known as the Coushatta Massacre. One body was reportedly so mutilated that it could barely be kept together during internment.[6] Two years later, in 1876, Twitchell survived an assassination attempt so serious that both of his arms had to be amputated.

Along with violence, the White League continued the racist campaign of the Ku Klux Klan. "Let the glorious wave of White Supremacy roll on to whiten and purify," proclaimed a Mississippi editor speaking for the White League. A league chapter in Winn Parish, Louisiana (the future birthplace of Huey Long), similarly resolved that "it was the intention of the founders of this Government that this should be a White Man's Government." The Franklin *Enterprise* explained the peculiar logic of racial superiority: "Science, literature, history, art, civilization, and law belong to us, and not to the negroes. They have no record but barbarism and idolatry, nothing since the war but that of war, incapacity, beastliness and crime." The ideology of white supremacy was set forth with clarity and power in an editorial in the Alexandria *Caucasian* entitled "The Negro—His Past and Future." Echoing racial attitudes that had served Southern whites since the Revolution, the editor stated that the black man was a "mere savage when left to himself, with the lowest instincts." The roots of black inferiority lay deep in the past. Africa was "without a history." Even its traditions "tell no story of a negro hero." This Southern editor constructed a timeless racial identity. In his eyes, the African American was "the same today that he was 3000 years ago, without letters, without art, without science and without a government." The inherent inferiority of the African American, according to this racial—and racist—logic, justified the subordination of the black race. Slavery had thus been a blessing for the African for it "left him clothed and in his right mind and upon the threshold of civilization." The close proximity of the races, albeit in an unequal relationship, would continue to prove beneficial to blacks. Around whites, blacks "heard and saw all that was intelligent and elegant in Southern life."[7]

The White League's recourse to violence and its ideology of white supremacy underscore its similarities to the Ku Klux Klan. The continuity did not go unnoticed at the time. The editor of the Alexandria *Caucasian* pointed out that Northern journals "are beginning to speak of the White Man's Party in the same manner, declaring it to be the remnants of the bloody spirit of Ku-Kluxism, disloyalty, etc." The leading Republican journal in Mississippi, the *Weekly Mississippi Pilot*, described the White League as "an oath-bound secret organization." Many historians have followed the lead of these editors of the 1870s, lumping the White League in with the Klan and the Knights of the White Camelia in a long line of post–Civil War violence. In his documentary collection of Reconstruction sources, for instance, Walter L. Fleming terms the White League chapters of Louisiana as "later manifestations of the Ku Klux movement."[8]

Yet the White Leagues differed in at least three significant ways from the Ku Klux Klan. First, they operated publicly, in the open. They did not employ the practices and rituals of secrecy so characteristic of the Klan. William A. Dunning, a biased but nonetheless astute twentieth-century student of Reconstruction, insisted that the local White Leagues "were distinct from the earlier order in maintaining little of mystery as to their doings and purposes." In 1874, a Louisiana editor sympathetic to the league explained "that here the White Man's Party is no secret organization and has no ritual."

The White League's widespread use of print culture in its campaigns was a second dissimilarity between it and the Ku Klux Klan. Several newspapers, such as the Alexandria *Caucasian* and the Natchitoches *Vindicator*, appeared simultaneously with the beginning of the White League movement in Louisiana. In fact, newspapers and their editors often played leadership roles in the movement. During the summer of 1874, when league organization was on the rise, the *Daily Shreveport Times* assumed the role of calling for a convention, "believing that we are giving expression, shape, authority, and circulation to the wishes of the white people of the State."[9]

Finally, the version of racial supremacy advanced by the White League had been significantly transformed since the time of the Ku Klux Klan. White League newspapers and spokesmen expressed what historians call the New Departure in Southern Democratic strategies, an acceptance of the constitutional amendments providing civil rights for African Americans. "We do not propose," explained the Alexandria *Caucasian*, "to interfere with any of the rights of the colored man nor drive him from us." In calling a mass meeting in Rapides Parish, the White League declared similarly (and perhaps equally disingenuously) that its members did not intend to deprive the black man of "any one of the rights secured to him by the Constitution and Laws," while the editor of the *People's Vindicator*, another White League newspaper, offered what he called the "right hand of fellowship" to African Americans. The New Departure was a product of the later years of Reconstruction, after the Grant administration had actively attacked and subdued the extremist measures of the Ku Klux Klan. It was a Democratic attempt to return to power through moderation, reconciliation, and an acceptance of the results of the Civil War. Of course, New Departure rhetoric was often hollow, as its adherents still wanted to keep African Americans out of politics.[10]

How can these differences between the Ku Klux Klan and the White League be explained? Part of the answer lies in chronology. Simply, the context for racial violence had changed significantly between the late 1860s and the mid-1870s. Factionalism within the Southern Republican Party and economic problems caused by the depression of 1873 had seriously weakened Republican governments and the appeal of Reconstruction among Southern whites. Moreover, the White League movement built on growing dissatisfaction with specific measures of the Kellogg administration in Louisiana, like the Returning Board and Registration Law of 1874, which the *New Orleans Bulletin* labeled "the most monstrous attempt to gag and manacle the free citizens of Louisiana."[11]

Still, the differences between the Ku Klux Klan and White League belie the notion of a uniform strand of white supremacy during Reconstruction. If post–Civil War racial violence was not monolithic, should historians be asking new questions about groups like the White League? How significant were time and place in shaping racial violence? More specifically, how did shifting political, social, and economic conditions influence the strategy and tactics of white opponents of Republican Reconstruction? What other grievances might have been incorporated into or masked by campaigns of white supremacy? White League newspapers offer a valuable source for pursuing these questions. My own examination reveals far more than a preoccupation with white supremacy and the evils of Republican Reconstruction. Two themes in particular stand out. The first is a disillusionment with political partisanship and a serious questioning of the social bases of Southern politics. The second is a rural distrust of urban, machine-dominated politics and consequent demands for a more inclusive political sphere. These two strains of White League thought suggest that the mid-1870s were a transitional period, not only marking the end of Reconstruction but also the visible outlines of the kind of social and economic dissent that defined the politics of the "New South."[12]

White League writings evinced a strong strain of agrarianism. A supporter of the movement from Caledonia, Mississippi, called himself "a voice from the unpretentious rural districts." As the White League was taking shape in Louisiana, A. L. Tucker of St. Mary's Parish expressed his beliefs as a "COUNTRY SENTIMENT." The Alexandria *Caucasian* even referred to its readers as "'country bumpkins.'" Such identifications reinforce the common understanding that the White League movement had strong support from rural areas in Louisiana. In June 1874, the New Orleans *Daily Picayune* reported that White Leagues were being formed in "country parishes." The league was strong in the northern part of the state and in the parishes along the Texas and Arkansas borders.[13]

Rural White Leaguers expressed an especially strong resentment against political domination by New Orleans. "There is no room for doubt," stated the New Orleans *Daily Picayune*, "that the city and country are, under existing circumstances, utterly at variance with each other." Farmers and planters in rural parishes and counties saw the White League movement as an opportunity for greater political inclusion, hinting strongly at longstanding feelings of exclusion. "The country," insisted the editors of the Alexandria *Caucasian*, "is determined to be heard and recognized in the interest of the White Man's Party." An emerging political movement based on whiteness seemed to offer poorer farmers a greater chance of equality. The Hon. A. L. Tucker called for an inclusive political organization "which admits within its fold all members of the white family of men who are disposed to cast their lot with their own race in this emergency." The editors of a rural White League newspaper called for the party convention to be held in Alexandria rather than in New Orleans.[14] This voice of agrarian protest in White League writings undoubtedly reflected the economic distress that plagued farmers across the cotton South during the 1870s. In Louisiana, the persistence of large landholdings after the Civil War created a steady growth of tenancy for both black and white farmers. The depression of 1873 hit Louisiana hard. "We once had plenty of money," explained one Louisiana planter in 1877, "but now the 'golden fleece' has departed and even our mule market is a poor one." Periodic flooding and a diversion of trade from New Orleans to Texas aggravated these other problems.[15]

In the second major theme, White Leaguers tended to characterize themselves as "a people's movement, independent of all past party affiliations and regardless of all past party names and organizations." The Alexandria *Caucasian* regarded the White Man's Party as "the people in their grand uprising" who could no longer be confined "to old party names and prejudices." White League leaders contrasted the populist dimension of their revolt to the political establishment. Another Louisiana editor claimed that the White League arose from the ashes of the "follies and failures" of the established parties. Several White League leaders mounted an explicit attack on the Democratic Party, insisting that it was a political machine that not only had failed to stem the tide of Radical Republicanism but also had become unresponsive to the popular will. By the summer of 1874, White League dissidents were calling for a white man's convention that would not be dominated by the regular Democrats. The editor of the Brashear *News* explained that "it is time for the Democratic leaders to give way to the loud and strengthening demand for a convention over which no party chief will preside; at which no party measure will be considered, into which no party tradition will enter." The pressure of the White League in the parishes forced the New Orleans Democrats to agree to a state convention in Baton Rouge in August 1874. This hostility to established party practices was expressed in the opposition to the convention system and in calls for open primaries. In Mississippi in 1875, primary elections were introduced for nominating local Democratic candidates.[16]

These two themes in White League writings anticipate the ideology of late nineteenth-century Southern agrarian dissent. In the 1870s, the Grange (formally the Patrons of Husbandry, founded in 1867) spread across the Midwest and South. The first Grange in Louisiana was organized in Jefferson Parish in March 1872. By 1875, 44 parishes in Louisiana boasted Grange chapters. White Leagues newspapers carried many notices about the Grange. As the Grange declined in importance, agrarian protest was rechanneled through the Farmer's Union, founded in Lincoln Parish in 1885. By 1891, there were 529 local unions in Louisiana. The Farmer's Union was strongest in northern Louisiana, an area that had long nursed grievances against the sugar parishes to be found in the southern part of the state. Throughout the New South, farmers challenged the planter and business interests that had secured hegemony of the Democratic Party. At various points, farmers were joined by factions of the Republican Party, Greenbackers, Knights of Labor, and Independents. In 1879, New Orleans citizens chafing under the rule of city bosses created the Anti-Ring Democratic Association. Agrarian unrest culminated, of course, in the populist movement of the 1890s.[17]

Along with agrarianism and a distrust of existing political structures, the White League shared with the agrarian movements of the late nineteenth-century grievances against privilege, corruption, economic hardship, and class oppression. During this period, Southern Democratic leaders were forced to confront, placate, or defeat insurgent movements from Southern white farmers and laborers. New South governments, as C. Vann Woodward argued in *Origins of the New South,* exhibited a "pervading distrust of the electorate and of popular government." Elements of this larger national retreat from democracy can be glimpsed in the many taxpayer's associations that sprang up in Louisiana, Mississippi, Texas, and South Carolina toward the end of Reconstruction. Even the Alexandria *Caucasian,* a newspaper arising in tandem with the White League, not only criticized Democratic elites but also insisted that the primary motive of Radical Republicanism in the South had been the exclusion of "the intelligent tax payers" from political office.[18]

Geography provides a more compelling link between the White League movement and agrarian protest in Louisiana during the 1880s and 1890s. Both movements seem to have flourished in the northern part of the state. In 1874, the Minden *Democrat*, a north Louisiana newspaper, estimated that at least ten thousand men in that part of the state were active in the White League. In 1884, the Republican candidate for governor carried four parishes in the north. There were even closer connections between Grant Parish, which bordered Rapides Parish (the county home of Alexandria), and agrarian radicalism. In the 1880s, an active branch of the Louisiana Farmer's Union (LFU) operated in the parish. In fact, Donna Barnes, a recent scholar of agrarianism in Louisiana, calls the parish an LFU "stronghold." Not surprisingly, populism was also strong in Grant Parish. Grant was one of six parishes in the state that gave a majority to the Republican–Populist Party coalition in 1892. For our purposes, it might also be suggestive that Alexandria was both home to the newspaper *Caucasian* and the birthplace of the People's Party in 1891. Indeed, leaders of the Louisiana Farmer's Union called the sheet "a paper that is worthy of our warmest support."[19]

There is also evidence that the racism so deeply embodied in the White League survived into the agrarian crusades of the late nineteenth century. This continuity can be illustrated through the career of Thomas Hickman of Grant Parish. Hickman was clearly involved in the Colfax Massacre of 1873, which hastened the collapse of Radical Reconstruction in the South. A decade later, Hickman was a member of Grant Parish's LFU.[20]

Yet we must be careful in rushing too soon into regarding the White League as a form of embryonic populism, for there were significant differences between the two as well. The agenda of the Alliances and People's Party, calling for cooperative buying, merchant lien laws, railroad regulation, and the subtreasury plan, did not appear in White League writings. Moreover, some Southern populists did invite the participation of black farmers, while the White League sought to block black participation in politics.[21] Furthermore, the White League was not exclusively a rural phenomenon. New Orleans boasted very strong urban chapters of the White League, based around the Crescent City Democratic Club, a paramilitary group formed in 1868 to counter Radical Reconstruction. Its constitution was similar to those of the rural parishes. New Orleans White League chapters took the leading role in the attempt to oust Louisiana's Republican government in the infamous Battle of Liberty Place on September 14, 1874. By that day, the commander of White League forces had enrolled twenty-six companies of infantry.[22]

This interpretation of the White League, admittedly tentative, still presents a possibility for revisiting two orthodoxies of Reconstruction and Southern historiography. First, it suggests that the traditional chronological boundaries of Reconstruction, 1865 and 1877, have obscured a perhaps more fundamental reorientation of Southern society and politics. The 1870s—encompassing agrarian unrest, labor conflict, and an economic depression—might well be considered as much a prelude to populism as an epilogue to Reconstruction. Second, the history of the White League might also lead us to reconsider the dynamics of race and class in Southern history. We have long been told that class conflict among whites in the South could be successfully muted by racist appeals to white supremacy. The history of the White League in Louisiana hints at a contrary interpretation—that racially motivated campaigns in the South might well have opened the possibility for whites to challenge an entrenched ruling elite.

Notes

1. Qtd. in John A. Garraty, *The American Nation: A History of the United States* (New York: Harper and Row, 1966), 303; James S. Allen, *Reconstruction: The Battle for Democracy, 1865–1876* (New York: International Publishers, 1937). For the nascent progressivism at the end of the century, see Jane Addams, *Democracy and Social Ethics*, ed. Anne Frior Scott (Cambridge, Mass.: Belknap Press of Harvard Univ. Press, 1964), 6. The rise of democracy in the United States during the nineteenth century can be traced through three recent books: Gordon S. Wood, *Empire for Liberty: A History of the Early Republic, 1789–1815* (New York: Oxford Univ. Press, 2009); Daniel Walker Howe, *What Hath God Wrought: The Transformation of America, 1815–1848* (New York: Oxford Univ. Press, 2007); and Sean Wilentz, *The Rise of American Democracy: Jefferson to Lincoln* (New York: W. W. Norton, 2005).

2. Qtd. in Mitchell Snay, *Fenians, Freedmen, and Southern Whites: Race and Nationality in the Era of Reconstruction* (Baton Rouge: Louisiana State Univ. Press, 2007), 167–68. In his book, *The Monied Metropolis: New York City and the Consolidation of the American Bourgeoisie, 1850–1896* (New York: Cambridge Univ. Press, 2001), Sven Beckert skillfully documents the antidemocratic impulse in the second half of the nineteenth century.

3. The literature on race, class, and democracy in the nineteenth-century South is vast. The starting point still needs to be Edmund S. Morgan, *American Slavery, American Freedom: The Ordeal of Colonial Virginia* (New York: Norton, 1975). For the antebellum era, see especially J. Mills Thornton III, *Politics and Power in a Slave Society: Alabama, 1800–1860* (Baton Rouge: Louisiana State Univ. Press, 1977); Lacy K. Ford, *Deliver Us from Evil: The Slavery Question in the Old South* (New York: Oxford Univ. Press, 2009); and George Fredrickson, *The Black Image in the White Mind: The Debate on Afro-American Character and Destiny, 1817–1914* (New York: Harper and Row, 1971). See also William W. Freehling, "The Divided South, Democracy's Limitations, and the Causes of the Peculiarly North American Civil War," in his *The Reintegration of American History: Slavery and the Civil War* (New York: Oxford Univ. Press, 1994). For the postbellum era, the place to start remains C. Vann Woodward, *Origins of the New South, 1877–1913* (Baton Rouge: Louisiana State Univ. Press, 1951).

4. Two classics in Reconstruction historiography recognize the problems of democracy in Reconstruction; see W. E. B. Du Bois, *Black Reconstruction in America, 1860–1880* (1935; rpt.,

New York: Atheneum, 1975); and Eric Foner, *Reconstruction: America's Unfinished Revolution, 1863–1877* (New York: Harper and Row, 1988).

5. Joe Gray Taylor, *Louisiana Reconstructed, 1863–1877* (Baton Rouge: Louisiana State Univ. Press, 1974), 285; E. T. Lewis, "The White League" (letter), *Caucasian* (Alexandria, La.), May 23, 1874 (quote); "Affairs in Louisiana," Senate Executive Document No. 13, 42nd Congress, 2nd Session, 30; Foner, *Reconstruction*, 550–51. The White Leagues are treated most fully in histories of Louisiana Reconstruction; see, for example, Taylor, *Louisiana Reconstructed*; Ella Lonn, *Reconstruction in Louisiana after 1868* (New York: Columbia Univ. Press, 1918); and Ted Tunnell, *Crucible of Reconstruction: War, Radicalism, and Race in Louisiana, 1862–1877* (Baton Rouge: Louisiana State Univ. Press, 1984). They are also discussed in Nicholas Lemann, *Redemption: The Last Battle of the Civil War* (New York: Farrar, Straus, and Giroux, 2006). The fullest study remains the essay by Oscar Lestage Jr., "The White League in Louisiana and its Participation in Reconstruction Riots," *Louisiana Historical Quarterly* 18 (1935): 617–95. On White Leagues in Mississippi, see William C. Harris, *Day of the Carpetbagger: Radical Reconstruction in Mississippi* (Baton Rouge: Louisiana State Univ. Press, 1979), 205, 677, 686; and *Weekly Mississippi Pilot* (Jackson, Miss.), Jan. 9, 1875.

6. Tunnell, *Crucible of Reconstruction*, 199, 194–201. See also his biography of Marshall Twitchell, *Edge of the Sword: The Ordeal of Carpetbagger Marshall H. Twitchell in the Civil War and Reconstruction* (Baton Rouge: Louisiana State Univ. Press, 2001); and Twitchell's autobiography, edited by Tunnell, *Carpetbagger from Vermont: The Autobiography of Marshall Harvey Twitchell* (Baton Rouge: Louisiana State Univ. Press, 1989).

Historian James Hogue has recently argued that "the White Leagues became the unofficial paramilitary wing of the Conservative/Democratic Party at a time of intense political crisis." Hogue, *Uncivil War: Five New Orleans Street Battles and the Rise and Fall of Radical Reconstruction* (Baton Rouge: Louisiana State Univ. Press, 2006), 126.

7. *Star of Pascagoula* (Pascagoula, Miss.), Aug. 8, 1874; *Caucasian* (Alexandria, La.), July 25, 1874; "Affairs in Louisiana," 31; *Caucasian* (Alexandria, La.), May 2, 1874. Forrest Wood's *Black Scare: The Racist Response to Emancipation and Reconstruction* (Berkeley: Univ. of California Press, 1968), remains a useful survey of the racial attitudes of white Southerners. See also Dan C. Carter, *When the War Was Over: The Failure of Self-Reconstruction in the South, 1865–1867* (Baton Rouge: Louisiana State Univ. Press, 1985).

8. *Caucasian* (Alexandria, La.), Aug. 1, 1874; *Weekly Mississippi Pilot* (Jackson, Miss.), Jan. 2, 1875; Walter L. Fleming, *Documentary History of Reconstruction: Political, Military, Social, Religious, Education, and Industrial, 1865–1906* (1907; rpt., New York: McGraw-Hill, 1966), 2: 327.

9. William A. Dunning, *Reconstruction, Political and Economic, 1865–1877* (1907; rpt., New York: Harper and Row, 1962), 269; *Daily Shreveport Times* (Shreveport, La.), Aug. 7, 1874; *New York Times*, Oct. 6, 1874; *Weekly Mississippi Pilot* (Jackson, Miss.), Jan. 16, 1875; *Shreveport Times* (Shreveport, La.), qtd. in the *Caucasian* (Alexandria, La.), July 25, 1874.

10. *Caucasian* (Alexandria, La.), Apr. 25, 1874, Aug. 15, 1874; *People's Vindicator* (Natchitoches, La.), Nov. 4, 1876, qtd. in William Ivy Hair, *Bourbonism and Agrarian Protest: Louisiana Politics, 1877–1900* (Baton Rouge: Louisiana State Univ. Press, 1969), 4. For further evidence of the acceptance of the Reconstruction amendments, see the *Daily Shreveport Times* (Shreveport, La.), Aug. 9, 12, and 15, 1874; and E. T. Lewis, "The White League" (letter), *Caucasian* (Alexandria, La.), May 23, 1874. The best introduction to the Democratic Party's New Departure strategy, introduced toward the end of Reconstruction, remains Michael

Perman's *The Road to Redemption: Southern Politics, 1869–1879* (Baton Rouge: Louisiana State Univ. Press, 1984).

11. "The Registration Law," *New Orleans Bulletin,* July 28, 1874, qtd. in the *Daily Shreveport Times* (Shreveport, La.), July 31, 1874.

12. On the significance of chronology *within* Reconstruction, see John Hope Franklin, *Reconstruction after the Civil War,* 2nd ed. (Chicago: Univ. of Chicago Press, 1994), 153; and David Herbert Donald, Jean Harvey Baker, and Michael F. Holt, *The Civil War and Reconstruction* (New York: W. W. Norton, 2001), 603.

13. *Columbus* (Miss.) *Weekly Index,* July 16, 1875; *Daily Picayune* (New Orleans, La.), July 22, 1874; *Caucasian* (Alexandria, La.), June 27, 1874, and June 20, 1876; "Affairs in Louisiana," 11.

14. *Daily Picayune* (New Orleans, La.), July 17, 1874, qtd. in the *Caucasian* (Alexandria, La.), July 25, 1874, 3; editors of the *Caucasian,* qtd. in the same issue, 2; A. L. Tucker, qtd. in the *Opelousas Courier* (Opelousas, La.), Aug. 1, 1874, 1.

15. John A. Buckner to Hubbard (G. Buckner?), Jan. 20, 1877, Buckner Family Papers, Filson Club Historical Society, Louisville, Ky.

16. *Caucasian* (Alexandria, La.), Aug. 15, 1874, 2, Aug. 22, 1874, 2; *Daily Picayune* (New Orleans, La.), July 17, 1874, qtd. in the *Caucasian* (Alexandria, La.), July 25, 1874, 3; *Brashear News,* qtd. in the *Caucasian* (Alexandria, La.), Aug. 1, 1874; Taylor, *Louisiana Reconstructed,* 297; Harris, *Day of the Carpetbagger,* 675.

17. Lucia Elizabeth Daniel, "The Louisiana People's Party," *Louisiana Historical Quarterly* 26 (Oct. 1943): 1063; Henry C. Dethloff, "The Alliance and the Lottery: Farmers Try for the Sweepstakes," *Louisiana History* 6, no. 2 (Spring 1965): 146–47; Matthew J. Schott, "Class Conflict in Louisiana Voting since 1877: Some New Perspectives," *Louisiana History* 12, no. 2 (Spring 1971): 159; Marguerite T. Leach, "The Aftermath of Reconstruction in Louisiana," *Louisiana Historical Quarterly* 32 (July 1949): 675.

On White League support of the Grange, see the *Caucasian* (Alexandria, La.), Apr. 11, May 9, and July 25, 1874; and the *Columbus* (Miss.) *Weekly Index,* July 16, 1875. On the Granger movement in the postbellum South, see Theodore Saloutos, "The Grange in the South, 1870–1877," *Journal of Southern History* 19, no. 4 (Nov. 1953): 473–87; and James S. Ferguson, "The Grange and Farmer Education in Mississippi," *Journal of Southern History* 8, no. 4 (Nov. 1942): 497–512.

Woodward, *Origins of the New South,* remains the essential starting point for studying agrarian protest and third-party movements in the postbellum South. Also valuable are Michael R. Hyman, *The Anti-Redeemers: Hill-Country Political Dissenters in the Lower South from Redemption to Populism* (Baton Rouge: Louisiana State Univ. Press, 1990); and Mathew Hild, *Greenbackers, Knights of Labor, and Populists: Farmer-Labor Insurgency in the Late-Nineteenth Century South* (Athens: Univ. of Georgia Press, 2007).

18. Woodward, *Origins of the New South,* 346; *Caucasian* (Alexandria, La.), May 9, 1874. On taxpayer movements in the late Reconstruction South, see Snay, *Fenians, Freedmen, and Southern Whites,* 168–69.

19. Hair, *Bourbonism and Agrarian Protest,* 199; Donna Barnes, *The Louisiana Populist Movement, 1881–1900* (Baton Rouge: Louisiana State Univ. Press, 2011), 66, 71; Dethloff, "The Alliance and the Lottery," 147; qtd. in Barnes, *Louisiana Populist Movement,* 98.

20. Barnes, *Louisiana Populist Movement,* 99. It should be acknowledged, however, that the Louisiana Farmers Union did contain some agrarian leaders, like Benjamin Brian and his son Hardy Brian, who pushed for interracial alliances between black and white farmers in Grant

Parish. On blacks in the Populist movement, see especially Gerald H. Gaither, *Blacks and the Populist Revolt: Ballots and Bigotry in the "New South"* (Tuscaloosa: Univ. of Alabama Press, 1977). Historians have long debated the extent to which Southern populism represented a genuine attempt a biracial democratic coalition. For some examples, see C. Vann Woodward, "Tom Watson and the Negro in Agrarian Politics," *Journal of Southern History* 4, no. 1 (Feb. 1938): 14–33; Charles Crowe, "Tom Watson, Populists and Blacks Reconsidered," *Journal of Negro History* 55, no. 2 (Apr. 1970): 99–116; and Lawrence Goodwin, "Populist Dreams and Negro Rights: East Texas as a Case Study," *American Historical Review* 76, no. 5 (Dec. 1971): 1435–36.

21. As is often the case, Woodward's *Origins of the New South,* especially chs. 8–10, remains the starting point for studying Southern populism. Major studies include Robert C. McMath, *Populist Vanguard: A History of the Southern Farmers' Alliance* (Chapel Hill: Univ. of North Carolina Press, 1975); Bruce C. Palmer, *"Man over Money:" The Southern Populist Critique of American Capitalism* (Chapel Hill: Univ. of North Carolina Press, 1980); Lawrence Goodwyn, *Democratic Promise: The Populist Movement in America* (New York: Oxford Univ. Press, 1976); Steven Hahn, *The Roots of Southern Populism: Yeoman Farmers and the Transformation of the Georgia Upcountry, 1850–1890* (New York: Oxford Univ. Press, 1983); and Charles Postel, *The Populist Vision* (New York: Oxford Univ. Press, 2007). For historiographical essays, see Patrick E. McLear, "The Agrarian Revolt in the South: A Historiographical Essay," *Louisiana Studies* 12, no. 2 (Summer 1973): 443–63; and James Turner, "Understanding the Populists," *Journal of American History* 67, no. 2 (Sept. 1980): 354–73.

22. Taylor, *Louisiana Reconstructed,* 283–84; Hogue, *Uncivil War,* 131–38. See also Foner, *Reconstruction,* 551.

Contributors

Kevin Adams is an associate professor of history at Kent State University, where he teaches a wide range of undergraduate and graduate courses in nineteenth-century American history. He received his Ph.D. at the University of California, Berkeley. Adams, a California native, is the author of *Class and Race in the Frontier Army: Military Life in the West, 1870–1890* (2009). He has also published book reviews, articles, and book chapters. Between 2010 and 2015, Adams served as the associate editor of *Civil War History*, the premier journal in the field.

Stanley Harrold received his Ph.D. at Kent State University. He is a professor of history at South Carolina State University in Orangeburg, where he teaches survey courses in American history as well as upper-division classes on U.S. Constitutional history, Colonial and Revolutionary America, and the Civil War and Reconstruction. He has written several books, including *Border War: Fighting over Slavery before the Civil War* (2010), which received the James A. Rawley Award, presented by the Southern Historical Association, as well as an honorable mention for the Lincoln Prize in 2011. Over the years, Harrold's research has been supported by fellowships from the National Endowment for the Humanities. Harrold is a frequent contributor of essays to journals and encyclopedias. His current project is a study of the effect of the abolitionist movement on the policies of the federal government during the eighteenth and nineteenth centuries.

Leonne M. Hudson received his Ph.D. at Kent State University, where he is an associate professor of history. He teaches several undergraduate and graduate courses in nineteenth-century United States history. He is the author of *The Odyssey of a Southerner: The Life and Times of Gustavus Woodson Smith* (1998) and the editor of *Company "A" Corps of Engineers, U.S.A., 1846–1848, in the Mexican War* (The Kent State

University Press, 2001). Hudson has penned several articles on the middle period and has written book chapters, encyclopedia essays, and book reviews. Hudson is currently working on a book-length manuscript on the reaction of black Americans to the death of Abraham Lincoln.

JOHN DAVID SMITH is the Charles H. Stone Distinguished Professor of American History at the University of North Carolina at Charlotte. He received his Ph.D. at the University of Kentucky and served as Fulbright Professor of American Studies at the Ludwig-Maximilians-Universität, München. Smith has written and edited numerous books, including most recently *We Ask Only for Even-Handed Justice: Black Voices from Reconstruction, 1865–1877* (2014) and *Soldiering for Freedom: How the Union Army Recruited, Trained, and Deployed the U.S. Colored Troops* (2014, with Bob Luke). He teaches many courses in nineteenth-century American history and serves as series editor for several university and commercial publishers.

MITCHELL SNAY is the former William T. Utter / Clyde E. Williams Professor of History at Denison University in Ohio, where he teaches several courses in nineteenth-century American history. Before coming to Denison, he was a lecturer in history and literature at Harvard University. The Chicago native received his Ph.D. at Brandeis University. He is the author of several books, including *Horace Greeley and the Politics of Reform in Nineteenth-Century America* (2011).

FAY A. YARBROUGH received her Ph.D. at Emory University and now teaches at Rice University in Houston, Texas. Before coming to Rice, she taught at the University of Oklahoma. Yarbrough is an associate professor of history who teaches a number of courses in nineteenth-century American history. In 2008, she published *Race and the Cherokee Nation: Sovereignty in the Nineteenth Century.* She was coeditor, with Sandra Slater, of *Gender and Sexuality in Indigenous North America, 1400–1850* in 2011. Yarbrough is currently working on a study of the participation of Choctaw Indians in the Civil War.

Index

U.S. War Department, military emancipation and, 27, 39

Venet, Wendy Hamond, 20
Vindicator (Natchitoches, Louisiana), 86
violence: abolitionist tactics and debate about, 6–10, 11–12, 15, 16–21; *posse comitatus* and, 68, 70–71, 72–74, 76; White Leagues and, 85–87
Vorenberg, Michael, 34, 67
Voting Rights Act of 1965, 18

Walker, David, 7
Wallace, George, 18
Walters, Ronald G., 6
War of 1812, black soldiers in, 30
Washington, George, 30
Weekly Mississippi Pilot, 86
Weld, Angelina Grimké, 8

Weld, Theodore, 9, 12
Welles, Gideon, 38
West Wing (television show), 66
White, Leonard, 66
White Leagues of Louisiana, 83–94; ideology of, 85–86; inception of, 84–87; overview, 5, 83–84; as populist movement, 88–91; in rural areas of Louisiana, 88, 89–91
Whitney, Eli, 7
Wilentz, Sean, 28, 33, 36, 37
Williams, Henry Llewellyn, 42–43
Women's National Loyal League, 20
women's rights, abolitionism and, 10, 17–18, 20
Woodward, C. Vann, 89
Wooster, Robert, 69
Wright, Elizure, 9
Wright, Henry C., 8, 12

Zouave Cadets, 30

Harrold, violent abolitionism led to
failure of equality cause.

Same w/ 1960s Ci. Rts mvmt
—Traces historians' understanding/
framing of abolitionists

Ⓧ Historiog. demonstrates: present
conditions influence historians'
assessment of CW/Recon effectiveness
of abolitionists
— Pessimism about the present
leads to conclusion that abols.
were ineffective

—Some 21st c. historians probing
viol/nonviol successes
— Present relation of social justice
to state power?